Crowdie and Cream

Crowdie and Cream

FINLAY J. MACDONALD

MACDONALD & CO
LONDON & SYDNEY

For Kathleen

First published in Great Britain in 1982 by
Macdonald & Co (Publishers) Ltd
London & Sydney

© Finlay J. Macdonald 1982

ISBN 0 356 08587 2

Filmset, printed and bound in Great Britain by
Hazell Watson & Viney Ltd, Aylesbury, Bucks

Macdonald & Co (Publishers) Ltd
Holywell House
Worship Street
London EC2A 2EN

Chapter One

'Big pee wet pussy' was, on the indisputable authority of my mother, the first reasonably coherent sentence that I ever uttered. If, nowadays, in translation it sounds like one of those dubious apothegms so indiscriminately attributed to Confucius, that is not, necessarily, further proof of my constant assertion that English is a very imprecise language compared with my own. At the time – given even that I was attempting to talk in our own native language – it was still only my mother's own complicity in the plot that made it possible for her to deduce from my apoplectic infant Gaelic that, despite all precautions, I had caught my father in the act of drowning the family cat in the peaty pool which he had fondly imagined to be out of sight of the house and of me.

My first sentence, unlike volumes of subsequent ones over the years, was a gross understatement. By the time I had scrambled my tearful way to the water's edge 'big pee' had not just 'wet pussy' but had rendered her very dead, and no amount of smooth baby-talk on my father's part would convince me that she was happier 'down among the lovely big water lilies' than she had been on his favourite chair or on my grandmother's knee. And it took me a long time to forgive my father, far less understand that in the commotion upon which we were embarking a cat of indeterminate pedigree was an encumbrance which he could well do without. In vain he tried to explain to me that the ducks and the drake, and the hens and the cockerel, and even Fanny, the sheep-dog, had to take precedence over the cat because they were going to help us make our way in our new life. Not that it mattered any more. By the time he finished talking the bubbles had slowed down and stopped . . .

We were, in fact, on the eve of uprooting and moving to a new world – a land bland and beckoning with promise – albeit only sixteen miles south. But, in those sixteen miles, a relentless rocky moorland gave way to flat green pasture fringed with golden beaches, and my parents were fortunate to be given the chance to make a new start with the best of their lives still ahead of them. Or so they must have thought.

I grew up with the legend that the Good Lord made the world in six days, and despite what people like Charles Darwin and David Attenborough have had to say on the subject that's the way that the bit of me I like best likes to believe it. If only for the tail end of the legend which goes on to say that when God was resting, as everybody should, on the seventh day, he suddenly discovered that he had completely forgotten to use one last handful of jewels which he had meant to place in some exotic area like the Caribbean. However, rather than break the Sabbath more than was necessary, he just opened a window in heaven and threw the jewels out without even bothering to watch where they fell. Some cynics claim that he still doesn't know but that, in fact, they strung themselves out along the north-west coast of Scotland forming the long line of islands now known as The Outer Hebrides.

I was born in the second island from the top. At least we call Harris an island, and even the Post Office calls it 'The Isle of Harris', but, geographically, it is only a tall mountain range which separates it from what is called, also inaccurately, the Island of Lewis. Be that as it may, a Harrisman is a Harrisman, and a Lewisman is a Lewisman, and neither would have it differently! Up till the end of the eighteenth century, Harris belonged to the Clan MacLeod whose Chiefs to this day call themselves the MacLeods of

6

Harris although their base is Dunvegan Castle in Skye. When the Clan system began to disintegrate during the eighteenth and nineteenth centuries Harris, like most of the other Clan Lands, was broken up and sold off to incomer landlords whose interests were either Sporting (in the hunting, salmon fishing or shooting sense) or Financial in terms of farming or commercial fishing.

Over the years the population was ruthlessly hounded off the rich arable land of the south-west and crowded on to the rocky heather shores of the northern and eastern coasts where the people squeezed bare livelihoods from thin soil and the sea. Their housing was primitive, consisting largely of thatched 'black houses' completely devoid of sanitation and custom designed for the encouragement of tuberculosis which was the inevitable death of one person out of three at the beginning of this century. Such cash as there was came from a haphazard cottage industry in Harris Tweed, and from family members who found work on the mainland or from the large numbers of men who went into the merchant navy.

Just after the First World War Harris received a rare injection of optimism when the whole island was bought by Lord Leverhulme, the multi-millionaire soap magnate, who had plans for the injection of massive capital into the island and its creation into the hub of a huge fish and tweed empire. Leverhulme's entrepreneurial genius had amassed him a fortune in the Congo, and the model town of Port Sunlight in Lancashire is still a monument to the enlightenment of his thinking and planning. Lord Leverhulme had already attempted to found mammoth fishing and agricultural projects in Lewis, but the deep-rooted suspicion of landlord intentions had denied him access to the free manipulation of the land resources which he regarded as fundamental to the integrated developments he envisaged. Frustrated by what he regarded as short-sighted intransigence, he abandoned Lewis and attempted to make a fresh start in Harris where the local population, who had had more time to study the 'Leverhulme vision', were much more willing to co-operate. Unfortunately Leverhulme died in the year that I was born and my father, who had been a staunch believer in him, was one of the many ex-servicemen who found themselves bogged down in the unrelenting past from which they had thought themselves to be escaping. After Leverhulme's death Harris was, once again, segmented into job lots of smaller estates and sold off to the highest bidders and it looked as if the old dreary pattern was about to be stamped once again on a community whose morale had suffered yet another collapse. But it wasn't to be quite like that. Although I – barely past the toddling period – could scarcely be expected to be aware of it, a whole new chapter of local history was beginning to be written around me, and it is typical of the innocent values of childhood that my vague awareness of it hinged on the drowning of a cat whose name or colour I can't even remember.

In 1919 a host of island soldiers and sailors had returned from the First World War eager to make a new start and get for themselves a share of the 'land fit for heroes to live in' which Lloyd George or someone in the elevated realms of government had promised them. That was all they wanted – for each a bit of land. They had been prepared to await the outcome of the Leverhulme experiment but when that bubble burst the old land hunger began to gnaw at them again. But too late. By the mid 1920s the nation's gratitude was beginning to ebb, and the new landlords who succeeded Leverhulme were not over-anxious to have their estates divided up among raggle-taggle warriors who didn't look nearly as impressive in threadbare pullovers and dungarees as they had done in uniform. And, come to think of it, they weren't nearly as necessary as they had been between 1914 and 1918 now that all the Peace Treaties were signed and sealed and more or less in the process of being ratified. But, over the years, a powerful 'crofter lobby' had been built up, and at last the Board of Agriculture in Edinburgh, which had already begun to show its teeth elsewhere, began to take a tentative interest in our neck of the woods.

My father and seven others were lucky. The landlord of a large and lush estate on the Atlantic coast of South Harris was prevailed upon to let a sizeable hunk of his territory be divided and rented out as eight crofts for which he would get annual rental while retaining to himself the fishing and shooting rights and, of course, the mineral rights should somebody stumble across gold. All the men had to do was pay their small rentals of about seven pounds a year, build themselves a village, and build, each to himself, a family of children and a flock of sheep in whichever order he chose. Much like Abraham and Jacob and Laban and those other forebears in another age and in another clime.

I wish I could remember and record some of the impact that my arrival, as the first boy of the new village, made on me. But, alas, all I can remember is that the two-hour journey in the little seven-seater bus which contained everything that we possessed in the world was punctuated by frequent stops for my mother to be sick. Poor woman! It was an affliction that was to bedevil her for years on the rare occasion that she made the journey. Nor was she by any means the only sufferer. The fact that the bus, with the springing of half a century ago, took two hours to complete a journey that is now comfortably achieved in a quarter of an hour is ample testimony to the state of a road which, in all fairness, was originally carved through the mountains for the occasional convenience of the traveller by horse and trap. But, over the years, it also became fairly obvious that my mother's upsets were always more pronounced on the journey south. Her heart never really left the Northlands, perhaps because her roots there were deeper than my father's. For someone of his strongly romantic nature the achievement of a place of his own in South Harris represented something akin to the emotion of the Jew returning to Israel; he was one of those people whose fairly immediate ancestors had been uprooted from the South during the evictions of the previous century and his sense of history could easily be manipulated to conjure up an imagery of an Israelite far, far older than the Jew. He was not to know that he was not escaping from bondage but, rather, going into it.

For me, the new village wove a spiritual and physical magic as I grew up with it. It was carved out from what had been the granary of the Clan MacLeod in the old days of that Clanship. The Atlantic thundered or shimmied according to its mood on mile upon mile of shell-white beach which, in its turn, was selvedge to rolling green meadowland intended, surely, by the Almighty in those early days of creation as a golf course. The machair, as it was called in Gaelic, was set aside as winter grazing for the township's sheep.

That was 'below the road', on the setting sun side. Above the road were the crofts themselves, each consisting of thirteen or fourteen acres of arable land stretching up to an infinity of heather moorland which was too rough and sour for cultivation but ideal for summer pasture. And the whole panorama was contained in a crescent swathe of tall mountains whose names, while ringing out like a peal of bells in Gaelic, in reality bore testimony to the Viking occupation of those lands a thousand years before. If it all sounds idyllic it's because it was to the boy who was I. And the land is still there for me to see when time allows me back to relive the years when it was moulding my life for me.

Our croft was probably the best of the eight in that the soil was a perfect blend of sand and peat through which the plough could shear an uninterrupted quarter-mile furrow; it was not by accident that the estate owners from the MacLeod Chiefs onwards had situated their vegetable gardens there. I know that only because Great Aunt Rachel once pointed out to me where the 'kale garden' as she called it had been, and Great Aunt Rachel would know because she was a relic of the indigenous population which had once thronged that coastline. She was my father's aunt, and by virtue of the fact that her people had been 'clerics' or clerks to the church there as far back as the eighteenth century, when the vast majority of the population had been shunted off to the Northlands during the evictions, her family had been allowed to stay on, on the moorland fringe of the church's land, in a 'grace and favour' hovel of stone and marram thatch. With that devout loyalty which the real 'Downstairs' has for the true blue 'Upstairs' Great Aunt Rachel never concealed the fact that she thought the nation to have fallen on evil days when fat rich lands were parcelled out to the peasantry.

In theory, thirteen acres of arable land, well cultivated, should provide enough vegetables and potatoes for the table and enough fodder for the cattle beasts in winter and they, in turn, should provide enough milk for drinking and for butter and cheese. By the same token the grazing outruns should maintain enough sheepstock to provide wool to make our clothes, mutton for the table and a small cash income from the sale of wethers and cast ewes to pay the rent. In addition to all that, our moorland grazing contained underneath it millions of tons of peat which would provide fuel for the crofting community for centuries and for free. Doubtless some ex-colonial bureaucrat, who had moved his desk from one of the crumbling outposts of Empire to Edinburgh, would add to all that bounty fish from the sea and rabbits from the machair for supplementary white meat and consider that a grateful government had done well by eight men returning from the trenches or the navy. And to a certain extent he would be right. Had our allocated corner of Utopia been in that particular bare-foot area of the Pacific for which God had meant those legendary jewels in the first place, then life for the settlers would have been superlatively good. For me and for the generation coming off the production lines it was good beyond measure in the early years, and when hardship came along – as it did – we were still too young to know it for what it was, and it's the *knowing* that makes the difference come joy, come sorrow.

11

Chapter Two

The view which opened up for us as we topped the Back of Scarista Hill on that first day can have done little to lift my mother's morale or confirm her faith in my father's optimism. As far as the eye could see there was nothing but beautiful emptiness save for the solid schoolhouse, built in 1892 when a rash of schools erupted through the West Highlands to conform to the Education Act of twenty years earlier, and an incongruously large church and manse dating back to the middle of the eighteenth century before the land had been cleared of its people. A few wisps of peat smoke from the moorland might have betrayed the well-camouflaged black houses of the few cottars who had been allowed to stay on in landless penury because they had proved too troublesome to evict or because they were useful as a supply of casual labour on the big estates. Finally, in the far distance ahead, there stood out in solitary splendour the small manorial homestead of Scaristaveg – the neighbouring estate which had escaped being crofterized. It was owned by a superficially benign old gentleman who had, at least, the virtue of being a Gaelic speaker from the mainland Highlands. But if those wisps of smoke from the moorland were visible from his drawing-room window he must have known that time was running out – fast!

Till such time as my father could get our house built we were to live with his Aunt Rachel – that redoubtable descendant of the clerics who had got out of her little

12

moorland cottage by dint of marrying a widower who had been himself employed by the church in some capacity or other in the days when part of the minister's 'living' was the sizeable swatch of prize agricultural land known as the glebe. Being allegedly committed to delving full time in Jehovah's vineyards the minister invariably employed at least one man to supervise the more earthly tillage. If Alastair was, indeed, such an employee he did very well out of it because he was able to provide Rachel with a large and comfortable home in a village only a few miles away from our new land. He appeared to make few demands on her – apparently not of the kind that resulted in a family anyway – and in exchange for looking after his daughter by his previous marriage, he indulged her to the extent of allowing her to bring our family to live under his roof for free and for as long as it might take my father to build a house. I have forgotten almost all of that period with the exception of our benefactress whom I was to come to love like a third grandmother.

Like all the women on the distaff side of my father's family, Great Aunt Rachel was built like a Churchill tank with a personality to match. She was also literate in that she could write and read English, which was not all that usual in her generation in our part of the world. And that, in itself, was enough to set her apart. She claimed to have met Lord Macaulay, which seemed to make a huge impression on people even though they had never heard of the great writer, and she could produce two crystal goblets which he had given her. All of which would seem to be perfectly feasible since the said Lord Macaulay's great grandfather had been minister of her old parish (the one we were about to enter into) and that reverend gentleman had carved himself a niche in eighteenth-century history by being the only man who tried to betray Bonnie Prince Charlie when the latter was being hunted in the Western Isles after Culloden. That particular bit of the story seemed to have escaped Aunt Rachel's capacious memory!

13

The crystal goblets were strictly for display and were only brought out to be polished or to be exhibited to some special visitor. They couldn't possibly be of any more practical use anyway in an environment as morally and economically stringent as hers, and they would have looked absurd with the thick black tea to which she was so thoroughly addicted.

No ancient or modern brewer of real ale was more devoted to his tipple than Aunt Rachel was to her tea. And no alchemist took greater care with the blending of his potions. She never used a teapot. She used a little black pan which she filled to within an inch of the top with fresh spring water and placed on the open fire so that it could absorb the flavour of the peat smoke that curled up around it as it came to the boil. When it began to bubble she added half a fistful of tea from a large caddy sporting a fading picture of Queen Victoria, whom, come to think of it, she resembled in more ways than one, and the brew was made to boil vigorously while she knitted a measured knuckle of sock which she had calculated long ago took her ten minutes. The fact that she got arthritic and slower as she got older didn't alter anything. As far as she was concerned an inch and a half of sock was still ten minutes, and that was the duration for which tea boiled. The tea got blacker as Great Aunt Rachel's hair got whiter, and she lived to be very old. Latterly her fainter-hearted visitors used to conjure up all sorts of excuses to get out of having to partake of her hospitality, and it was useless for her sister or her stepdaughter, who guessed at the reason for the reluctance, to suggest a milder distillation. But it was only well behind her back that anybody dared smile at the old lady's oft-quoted assertion – in which the pun evaded her innocence in both her languages – 'When I make tea I make tea, and when I make water I make water.'

Great Aunt Rachel was the repository of the history of her branch of our family – the only branch that counted in her reckoning – and it was she who told me, later on in life, how we all began and why I look the way I do.

It all went back to a sea battle between the English and the Spaniards 'away down in the south' according to her. And the English routed the Spaniards, which was just as it should be since there were no Scots in the opposing team. 'Round about the end of the sixteenth century' was the nearest she would come to putting a date on it. Anyway, the Spanish fleet was defeated and tried to escape back home by the long way round the north of Scotland, but they ran into heavy weather and most of their galleys foundered in the Orkneys and the Western Isles.

Round about that time a spinster fore-runner of ours was dragging out a lonely existence in a house on the very spot of moorland where Aunt Rachel's own home had stood before she married her widower, above what was to be our new village. The lady was approaching the age when matrimony seemed to be passing her by and she had to rely on her neighbours to cut her peat for her and keep her supplied with her minimal requirements of food in the way of milk and meat and oatmeal. She augmented her store of fuel by beachcombing when the wind was in the west, and it was after one particularly bad storm that she went down to the sands and found what she took at first to be a corpse bobbing in the ebb. 'She turned the thing over with her foot,' to use Great Aunt Rachel's own words, 'and, lo and behold, he stirred and groaned.' Being a kindly soul she took him home and dried him out, and he turned out to be – again I quote – 'a little sallow sailor from foreign parts who couldn't speak any Gaelic'. Which is not surprising if, as Aunt Rachel seemed to imply, he was a lone survivor from the ill-fated Armada of King Philip II of Spain! Anyway, the two got married and from them descended my Great Aunt Rachel and, in due course, me.

It was a great pedigree for a romantically inclined young boy like me to grow up with, and for years I was happy to attribute to it a complexion that is decidedly off-white and a *mañana* attitude to dead-lines. It was only recently that

15

– having been caught up in the frenetic slip-stream of *Roots* – I decided to put my past to the test and tentatively approached the distinguished Scottish genealogist, Bill Lawson, and asked him to confirm the legend. Bill is a man of infinite kindliness and nothing would have delighted him more than to give me a chart straight back to Mount Ararat, but his professional integrity would allow him only to confirm that my first known ancestor was one Murdo MacKay (*floruit* 1780) who was indeed shipwrecked on Toe-Head – a wild headland jutting into the Atlantic in front of our village. But that was two centuries after the Spanish Armada, and Murdo MacKay is one of the less likely Spanish names. What is more credible is that he was a survivor from the wreck of one of the ships bound for America with a cargo of the victims of one of the early infamous Sutherland Clearances – perhaps, indeed, a sole survivor. For sure there was such a man, and, having escaped with only a broken leg, he decided out of gratitude to the Almighty to devote his services to the church and he became the 'cleric' from whom Aunt Rachel was descended.

Since that encounter with the reality, I have become increasingly aware that every by-ordinar living being in the West Highlands, from unsociable marmalade tom-cats to the most vicious midges, are invariably debited, one way or another, to some form of flotsam from the Spanish Armada.

And Lord Macaulay's crystal goblets . . .? Well, they're there all right. But, even without recourse to any form of historian or other authority, I can deduce with reasonable certainty that Lord Macaulay was dead by the time Great Aunt Rachel was born. But I have noticed that always, somewhere, there was a grain of history in her fictions and, at worst, I like to think that she had a vivid imagination.

My father did not inherit the forcefulness of personality of 'the clerics'. He was a mild-mannered man who despite of – or, perhaps, because of – five gruelling years in the

16

trenches would go out of his way to avoid trouble or even an argument, choosing to take a quizzical view of life through the wrong end of the telescope. What he did inherit from them was a strong streak of imagination and poetry – qualities which were not, necessarily, the best assets for a man beginning to carve out a new living from raw croft land.

The pattern of procedure was that each new crofter built, on his land, a corrugated iron shack into which he moved with his wife and the beginnings of his family while he was building up his stock of sheep and cattle. My father started off in due course with one jet black cow, inexplicably called Daisy, and about twenty sheep donated by his own parents and his in-laws. The theory was that they would multiply and keep on multiplying till he achieved the regulation quota or 'souming' of sixty sheep and two cows and their followers. One only had to thumb back through Holy Writ to the Book of Genesis and the story of Noah to be reassured that spectacular results could be achieved with a considerably smaller, if more varied, investment of breeding stock than even my father had. And Noah didn't have the patronage of the Board of Agriculture for Scotland which had pledged itself to the provision of a pedigree bull who would be changed every two years to avoid any danger of incest.

Our 'pattern of procedure', however, seemed to be taking an unduly long time to establish itself and our new house a long time to materialize, although, by all the laws, we were enviably placed in that my mother came of a long line of carpenters – the extant members of which had volunteered to give of their services. In fact, for the first few years of our life in the south, we were to discover that our vaguest relatives from the Northlands were more than willing to come and share in our toils, particularly in summer, in much the same way as the modern city-dweller discovers clouds of unsuspected friends the moment he acquires a cottage in the country.

In the end, with another spring descending on us and

17

only the foundations of the new house laid, it was decided that it might be better to live on location, and so, along with another family, we moved into the residential end of the school building which was initially planned for the head-teacher's family, but which was vacant for reasons that I shall bring myself to describe later. We weren't to know that our short sojourn in the schoolhouse was to give us a ringside seat for events which were to reverberate throughout Scotland and raise echo in the Mother of Parliaments in Westminster.

Chapter Three

There is a highly distinctive odour of which whiffs may still, very occasionally, be detected in the corridors of the House of Lords, although never at Ascot. Like the most exclusive perfumes it is a harmonization of many essences and, nowadays, at the higher end of the olfactory register one may detect contributions from the distinguished palaces of Givenchy or Dior. But pervasively, and unmistakably to the cognoscenti, there comes through, on humid days in particular, the inter-reaction of wool and urine. To say that one is more likely to come across it among the older representatives of the aristocracy is not to suggest a higher incidence of incontinence among the hereditary members of the Upper Chamber. It is just that by virtue of their age and tradition they are more likely to be still the wearers of the real hand-spun, hand-woven, 'never-left-the-croft' Harris Tweed which was the mainstay of the primitive economy of the island at the time of which I write.

It was Lady Dunmore, the wife of one of the more enlightened former proprietors of Harris, who had seen the potential of the rough, tough, cloth made from the wool of the local black-face sheep as ideal cladding for the hunting, fishing and shooting fraternity which was beginning to discover the Western Isles at the beginning of the century. And she had encouraged the wives of her tenants to make tweed surplus to their own domestic requirements, and she had helped them to market it. In my young days we were still only in the early stages of adapting to a 'money economy' and the wives of cottars and crofters alike were just beginning to exploit their home-made tweeds as a source of hard cash to pay the rent and the increasing luxuries of imported food and clothes. Although my grandfather, on my father's side, was a weaver it was only after we had moved south that I became conscious of the paraphernalia of the trade – important among which was the pee-tub, to which I had first been introduced during our stay with Great Aunt Rachel.

When hand-spun Harris Tweed comes out of the loom it is very rough indeed, and very loose and greasy. It has to be shrunk to a pre-ordained width beyond which it is guaranteed to shrink no further on the wearer's back. Otherwise the results might be highly uncomfortable, if not strangulating in sundry places. The roughness is an acceptable, and indeed desirable, characteristic of the cloth since it contributes to the wearer's warmth and to his (or her) 'man-among-the-heather' image. But the greasy oiliness, which was part of the essential rain-proofing of a Hebridean sheep, was always considered more than even the most dedicated stalker or salmon fisher could tolerate, and it was partially removed during the shrinking and washing process.

The substance most effective for removing the oiliness was ammonia and – far removed as we were from hardware and chandlers' shops – the best available source of ammonia was matured human urine. Not only did it clean the tweed but it gave it that distinctive aroma about which the gentry from the Home Counties used to rave, and which, as I've said, may still be found to cling to those members of the monied classes who are aristocratic enough to be able to boast of old suits in which the *nouveau riche* would not be seen dead.

Anyway, for some time after we became established in the new village it was common for every household to save up its spent pennies, as it were, in large tubs in the byre or some sheltered place where the rain would not dilute the collection too much and interrupt its maturing. Every household contributed to its own tub as did friendly visitors who were doubly welcome if they happened to be breaking their journey on the long road home after a night on the beer. 'Where do you keep your tub?' was our nearest genteelism to 'Where can I wash my hands?' – that absurd euphemism which I have known to land many a bewildered tourist in a bedroom equipped with a ewer and a wash hand basin which far from fulfilled his most urgent need. In more sophisticated parts of the nation specialists in porcelain were making fortunes evolving quick methods for disposing of what we were struggling to save, but it was to be several years before they were to find a market with us.

During the few months of our stay in the schoolhouse we didn't have a pee-tub of our own, partly because my mother couldn't settle down to the business of spinning for a tweed till we got settled into our new house, and, largely, I suspect because the lady whose sub-tenants we were in a way would almost certainly have objected. For some reason best known to herself, the Headmistress, as she was called, although she was the sole representative of the Education Authority in the parish, chose to live in lodgings rather than in the schoolhouse which had been designed for a man with a family. For all I know the Authority may have moved her out in order to make room, temporarily, for us and the other family whose own house wasn't yet ready for occupation. In any case Miss Dalbeith roared out of the morning and into the evening on a motor-bicycle causing stampedes among the villagers' small herd of cows and horses which had not yet become accustomed to their new surroundings, far less the petrol-ized age and female motor-cyclists.

At that stage, mercifully, I had nothing to do with Miss Dalbeith nor, even more mercifully, had Miss Dalbeith anything to do with me. We heard a lot of her – through the schoolhouse wall – but, except for her arrivals and

21

departures, we saw little of her apart from her once-daily visit to inspect the house presumably to ensure that we weren't breaking up and burning the doors or the floorboards for fuel. Once or twice my father tried to engage her in conversation on the strength of being able to speak English and having himself once had a motor-bicycle, but he got short shrift and was left muttering to my mother that the lady was better suited to a broomstick. When she took to riding through the village occasionally on a Sunday, all the elders could do was wish that she were a member of the kirk so that she could be excommunicated. Miss Dalbeith would have been above the law even if the occupant of the Manse had been the Ayatollah Kerr instead of the Reverend . . .

I suspect that the only reason why I didn't stumble more across the path of my future 'Headmistress' was that I was revelling in the freedom of the wide-open spaces of the new village. Having lived till then amidst the sheltered rocky bays and inlets of the north, the explosion of space was overwhelming. I remember as if it were yesterday instead of half a century ago, standing alone – a minuscular fluff of infancy on an infinity of sand – staring at a sea horizon far out and above my eye level, picking up a distant swelling in the water which would move seemingly slowly and gently towards me but gathering weight and volume and power as it came, till, at last, it seemed to hang high above me with a white angry fringe forming on its top. And then it would crash down with a roar that picked up an echo from somewhere, and suddenly, as if defeated or tamed, it would end up like a fold of deckled creamy linen at my feet and then crease back whence it came. Often and often my mother would have to trek the whole width of the beach to drag me back home because no shouting voice could carry against the waves even on the quietest day. Poor woman! She had been brought up beside a sea without waves, and she never lost her fear of the Atlantic. Nor I my respect for it.

Some days I would set off in the other direction and

22

up towards the little black houses of the old population – old in the sense that their people had been there on the moor's edge for generations. In terms of years, the menfolk were only slightly older than my father. Although my father's people had been of their stock, they seemed different from us. Or perhaps the legend which surrounded them made them seem different to the little boy. Two of them had been in prison and, although I didn't know it, they were preparing to go again. One of them was a tall black shepherd who sang songs that he composed himself, and the other was alleged to be a joiner, although I never knew him to practise a trade. Their crime had been an attempt to stake out land for themselves from the small estate which lay adjacent to the one which had been allotted to us. And when they were arrested they had shown contempt not only for the law but also for the Court – in words and ribald song. They had been sentenced to four months in Porterfield Prison in Inverness, but Labour M.P.s led by Tom Johnstone (later to be Secretary of State for Scotland) created such a row that they had been allowed home after two months, and they had returned as folk heroes and utterly unrepentant.

I used to spend hours listening to the Black Shepherd telling his stories as he puffed incessantly at an evil-looking stubby pipe which he kept re-filling from a long rope of thick black tobacco sliced and rubbed to the correct texture between palms that rasped like two pieces of sandpaper. His wife was a tea maker of only marginally lower calibre than Great Aunt Rachel, and she plied it with a generosity which would have taxed the bladder of a seasoned drinker of Somerset cider than which there is no more impatient brew. Whenever I got up at nature's insistence I was reminded to be sure to 'use the tub now'. That tub had stood for so long that its fumes would have brought tears to the eyes of a seaman, and it was on the point of becoming the subject of a song which is now, to the best of my knowledge, in the archives of Edinburgh University.

The Black Shepherd was, in theory at least, an employee of the landlord who owned the estate which had been the centre of the troubles earlier on, but I suspect that he had been made redundant – to use a word which had not then acquired such common currency – following on his encounters with the law. Certainly he was never a guest in the house of the landlord who was basically a gentle character with only two passions in life – trout fishing and a card-game called 'catch-the-ten', which was a modified form of whist in which the object was to capture the ten-spot card of whichever suit was trump, or, as the landlord called it, 'trumph'. His guests, in the main, were chosen from among his more docile tenants and the incomer crofters because he wasn't sufficiently 'upper-crust' to merit the attention of the belted knights who were his fellow estate owners. Nor was 'catch-the-ten' sufficient intellectual challenge for the doctor and the minister. In any case he preferred his cronies to be 'trusties' whom he could depend upon to let him win, and who in their turn knew that if they didn't their chances of going home with a few plump trout were considerably diminished.

Up on the moor the Black Shepherd and his friends were getting restive. It says much for them – either that or it underlines a defeatism born of generations of repression – that they had accepted their reverses with so little rancour towards us, the incomers. They had watched the fat land on their doorsteps being parcelled out among strangers. They had seen the newcomers appearing to begin to prosper. They had seen one season of corn ripening and being harvested by men who had, perhaps, less claim to that particular land than themselves. And they were now beginning to see new houses going up while they were confined to their hovels. At last, while the spring nights were still long enough for the card sessions to be in progress the men from the moors decided to deal themselves a fresh hand and they were determined that they were going to deal themselves some trumps.

Over the weeks they had quietly procured some sacks of

grain, and one fine spring morning they went out and parcelled out some of the landlord's best fields among themselves and began to plough and sow. This time they had acted without warning, and there was no policeman on hand to stop them. Previously they had merely staked out claims to land, marking their claims with assorted little pegs, but now they they were planting seed. Needless to say, the landlord couldn't stand by and nod approval while his best green fields turned black under a plough of his own which had been commandeered from behind his steadings overnight, and, in those pre-telephone days, there was nothing he could do except drum up a regiment, in the shape of some reluctant farm hands, to drive off 'raiders' who were, in all probability, their own kith and kin. The farm hands, directed by the landlord waving a silver mounted walking-stick, went into action. But they had reckoned without the women!

Up on the hillside, the women-folk saw their men being 'attacked' by the landlord and his henchmen and they decided to take a hand. They formed a loose-knit human chain stretching from the pee-tubs to the landlord, and pail after pail of malodorous urine passed down the line to be generously thrown over the landlord who, alone, attempted to hold his ground. But not for long. Soaking wet, and with smarting eyes, he too was forced to retreat leaving the ploughmen to sow their grain to the last handful, cheered on by the school-children whom even Miss Dalbeith could not control. The law, of course, had to move against the 'raiders' once again, and, once again, the ringleaders went to prison to even greater press and parliamentary outcry than before. It would be nice to tell that the 'raiders' came out of jail to find fields of golden corn awaiting them. But, alas, no. And it was just as well for them that their sentences were in no way timed to the harvest.

In the short term nobody won. The landlord, having washed and disinfected himself, rubbed his hands glee-fully and proclaimed that his fields had been sown for him without cost to himself, and he set about the business of catching trout and playing 'catch-the-ten' with great content. What he didn't know – any more than they themselves knew – was that the cottars had lost their agricultural know-how somewhere along the line and what they had bought and sown by some inexplicable mischance was a large quantity of sago which did not flourish in our climate and our soil. The winter's imported cattle food cost the landlord dear.

There was one sad side-effect resulting in a change which, I suppose, would have come sooner or later anyway. As a result of the 'battle of the pails' there was an acute shortage of matured urine for tweed that year and an enterprising shop-keeper somewhere cashed in on it by importing bottled ammonia for the first time. For the pee-tub time was trickling out.

In those days, visitors to the village were few and far between. There were only a dozen or so cars on the whole island, and when during the daylight hours one or other of them ventured along the coastal track which was only then being carved out as a single track road, its noise could be heard approaching from a mile away. There was always a rush to windows and doors to see it pass, and it was good for half an hour's speculation as to who was in it and where it was going and why. If it happened to be the doctor's then the speculation would continue into the next day till it was established whether he was on his way to fish or to death. Speculation would end only on the arrival of Calum the Post who, whether he was delivering or collecting the mail, could be depended on to be carrying a greater volume of news in his head than in his van.

Occasionally, word would get round the community that 'men from the Board were coming round'. By what form of bush telegraph the news got round I do not know but, presumably, the visitors from the mainland would have had to make arrangements for the hiring of a car from Stornoway or Tarbert and the driver of the car would be an islander who had a sister who had a cousin who had a friend in the long line of word of mouth communication which has been the bush telegraph in rural areas the world over since tribal barriers were broken down and men could trust each other to pass on messages more accurately than smoke signals could do. Not so very long ago an old man who had been a boy on the remote island of Scarp, off the north-west coast of Harris, assured me that, before the First World War, at times when Scarp was cut off from the mainland of Harris by winter storms, news would reach Scarp of events which had taken place in the very south of Harris within twenty-four hours. It is no more puzzling than the fact that in our own micro-chip age there is still nothing that excels the speed of rumour.

The 'men from the Board' were dapper gentlemen who travelled in pairs and wore knickerbockers and brushed their teeth. They represented the Board of Agriculture which had been set up in 1912 with powers to acquire, compulsorily if necessary, some of the vast West Highland estates and divide them into crofts to satisfy the insatiable land hunger which was sweeping the whole of the north of Scotland. Its task was what an earlier Irish politician had described in similar circumstances as the 'unshirkable duty to strive towards undoing the unnatural divorce between the people and the land'. 'The people' were the contemporaries of my grandparents and parents in the north of Scotland as in Ireland – ordinary men and women as opposed to 'the lairds' or 'the landed gentry' who had been for generations their exploiters and oppressors to a degree unparalleled today save in the totalitarian states of South America.

'What is that floating in the ebb?' the old Highlander asked his crony. 'It looks like a board of wood or something.'

'If it is moving fast,' was the reply, 'it will *be* a plank of wood. If it's moving slowly it'll be the Board of Agriculture.'

The Board had, perforce, moved slowly over the twenty-five years or so of its existence, hampered less perhaps by

27

the interpolation of two wars than by the intransigence of landlords whose credo was 'to have and to hold', and who, in the upholding of that credo, were prepared to exploit every avenue of legality and appeal.

But, slowly, on the Highland mainland and in Skye and some of the other Hebridean islands the Board of Agriculture had inched on against the opposition and had created some two and a half thousand new crofts and enlarged more than five thousand previously established small - very small - holdings. In all, about three quarters of a million acres of land had had the 'unnatural divorce' healed and been given to the people. In the process, of course, the Board of Agriculture had, in the British fashion, inbred itself into a bureaucracy with its own laws and laws to safeguard its own laws, so that by the time our men, at the tail end of the line, were given their bit of land, a croft had, indeed, become 'a piece of land surrounded by regulations'. It was in the supervision of these regulations that the knickerbockered twosomes always planned to arrive on us unexpectedly.

It may well have been a Hebridean who coined the phrase: 'When the Good Lord made time, he made plenty of it.' And if it was, why not? But the chestnut has been hung round his neck to imply that the islander will not willingly do today what can be put off till tomorrow, and I am certainly not living proof to the contrary. But, in those boyhood days about which I'm writing, it was difficult, if not pointless, to cultivate a sense of urgency when life was governed by time and tide, by season and weather, and by communication and transport. Every stick of wood and every sheet of corrugated iron and every piece of ancillary hardware from shelf brackets to nails had to be imported – invariably from Glasgow or from Greenock, because it was from there that the venerable coasters *The Dunara Castle* and *The Hebrides* sailed on their Odysseys round the myriad islands of the west coast with us at the tail end. Certain shops and firms in those faraway places had near monopolies of our community's trade by virtue of the fact that they could interpret the islanders' needs as expressed in rough sketches and fractured English, and acted on them as expeditiously as the schedules of the two ships allowed. Some of those firms won themselves trust and loyalty which were to help swell their prestige and their profits for decades, and their names became part of the vernacular. For years I had to pause and think whether Peter Fisher was the Galilean apostle or the Glasgow supplier of paints and wallpapers.

But it mattered not how efficient the suppliers, their deliveries were still governed by the schedules of *The Dunara* and *The Heb*, and their schedules, in turn, were governed by tide and weather because, in those days, they had to unload at some very exposed rough jetties or even ferry their cargoes ashore in dribs and drabs by rowing boat. It could well be a month before an order despatched from our village was finally delivered, and it could well be that when it was delivered the weather had turned so stormy that only an idiot would attempt to manoeuvre a six-foot sheet of plywood or corrugated iron; or else the materials would appear on the very first day of a spell of dry weather which had to be seized upon for the cutting of the peat or the shearing of the sheep – whichever chore was seasonal at the time.

These were factors not always appreciated by the bureaucrats in Edinburgh whose morning coffees and afternoon teas arrived on their desks at the pre-ordained times regardless of whether or not *The Dunara Castle* was being held up in Castlebay for nine days by a force ten gale. And so, when the days were sufficiently lengthened and the salmon were deemed to be running well in the Outer Islands, the men from the Board tore themselves away from their offices and their wives and set out on their pilgrimages to check on the progress being made by the new crofters on the new land which had been bestowed upon them.

While the men from Edinburgh may not have understood the problems governing the tempo of island life, the men of the islands understood the official mentality fine.

As soon as news came that an inspection was imminent all the proper seasonal work was temporarily abandoned, and work on the new houses was resumed with vigour even if it meant stripping off some sarking or corrugated iron that had already been laid, and going through the motions of nailing it back on again. By whatever means, every man jack in the village was busy as the government's hired car jolted its way down the road, stopping here and there to justify its journey. Since a tour of the crofting communities was a coveted 'perk' for the office-bound officials, they came round in strict rotas so that, in fact, the same pair never came on successive occasions, making it extremely difficult for one delegation to decide whether or how much advance had been made on what had been seen by the previous one. The crofters, who could modulate the fluency of their English as the occasion demanded, were always cautiously reassuring. And, at the end of the inspection, they always wished the officials 'a nice holiday'. At which the men from the Board flashed uncertain little white smiles and continued their journey towards the hotel where, I am sure, they coined new aphorisms on the theme of God making plenty of time.

Chapter Four

Up till now I have written as if we were just three in our family. But we weren't. We were, in fact, four. Just before we left the Northlands my mother had – with consummate timing – provided my father with a second son and me with a first brother, three years to the day and almost to the hour after she had brought me into the world in unconscious celebration of America's Independence Day. He is now a hirsute hunk of middle-age whose arrival in a community, far less a room, can scarce pass unnoticed, but in the days of our transit encampment in the school-house he was too immobile to be of consequence or companionship.

My earliest companion was, in fact, a girl of neither kith nor kin. If I was the first of the incomer boys in the new village, then she was the first girl – older than me by a whiff of years which chivalry now forbids me measure publicly. Like me, she had been born furth of the village, and, like me, she was in a state of suspended domiciliation in the schoolhouse while her father, who treasured time as laconically as my own, was building their new tempor-ary house on a croft two miles along the road. There were four in her family too, and to this day I cannot figure out how eight people managed to crowd into the tiny school-house. But we did. And during the long summer holiday when she was free from the moils of Miss Dalbeith's class-room Molly and I became intermittently firm friends. It

31

says much for the soothing of time that we are friends still despite the fact that she is the only person who, to my knowledge, set out deliberately to poison me!

We had come from different but equally harsh and rocky areas of the island, and the freedom of the flat green miles and the white beaches must have been as overwhelming for her as for me. The lush coastal land had never known a chemical, nor predator worse than a leisurely cow, and so in summer it erupted with buttercups, daisies, speedwell, groundsel, yarrow, forget-me-nots and ones I've long since forgotten, or whose names I have never known in English. It is an occasionally regretted fact of life for me that I have two strictly limited botanical horizons. There is a vast flora with which I was familiar in boyhood, the terminology of which never seemed to merit being translated into the English area of my vocabulary upon which there always seemed to be more pressing demands, with the result that I can walk through the Chelsea Flower Show in exalted company and in moronic silence because a prize Iris Reticulata is, to me, common marshland 'sealasdair' which, when boiled with wool, gives a very distinctive black in the making of Harris Tweed. A foot in two cultures can be fulfilling at times and chastening at others.

But when one talks of cultures one is admitting to an awareness which is sometimes the very negation of culture in the real sense, and what Molly and I were revelling in was just the simple business of enjoying being alive in a good world to which we knew no alternative. In those days neither of us, nor any of our kind, wore shoes from May till September and there are few tingles that linger in the sub-conscious more delicately than those skiffing runs through the morning with daisy and buttercup heads clipping off between toes cold in the dew. To the boy and the girl those were the Eden days before the apple blushed.

I suspect that Molly's seniority occasionally made her impatient with the unrelieved company of a mere boy. Maybe deep below her own comprehendings there were the stirrings of the old primeval instinct to which the boy as yet held no key. Maybe the boy was just the surrogate rag doll – easy to pick up but difficult to discard at whim. Anyway, at times she would tire of me and on occasion she tried to lose me by using the superior speed of her lanky legs to strand me in the sand dunes far from the sight of home. But I had the homing instinct of a retriever pup and I was quick to learn that if I kept out of sight for a while and then arrived at the door looking bedraggled and blubbering and feigning terror I would get cuddled while Molly would get clouted for abandoning me to dangers which I have still to discover in that bland and empty land. Till one day she decided to get rid of me once and for all.

We were, she assured me, going to visit a secret place far beyond the limits of our normal peregrinations, and I was to tell no one. It was always flattering to be invited on an excursion with Molly and, in my innocence, it never dawned on me that the invitations came only at week-ends and during the school holiday when the two or three girls that there were of her own age retreated to their own patches all of three miles away. She had a sister who was in the same age relationship to her as my brother was to me, and, by that token the same age as me, but her sister was of a much less tom-boyish nature than Molly and, in any case, was more resistant to Molly's blandishments and blackmails because she had grown up in their shadow. So, we were given permission to set off with the usual warnings from the two mothers to Molly to look after me and to make sure that she didn't let me out of her sight. The warnings were as routine as were their disregardings.

We headed, as usual, in the direction of the beach and as soon as we reached the broad belt of marram grass that separated the grazing land from the shore Molly began to lengthen her considerable stride. This was an old dodge, but I always fell for it. As soon as I began to pump furiously to keep pace, the marram tips whipped at my bare calves like a myriad needles till I was gritting my teeth against the tears. And the more my vision blurred the more likely I came to stubbing my toes against the marram roots and stumbling. And the more I stumbled the more Molly taunted me with my footlessness and cried me on. I knew it was useless to shout 'Wait for me' and so I blundered on careful only to dodge the rabbit holes which I knew could wrench a knee or an ankle. Time blurred. But the anticipation of a 'secret place' spurred me on, and eventually I tumbled over the rim of a large green hollow at the bottom of which Molly sat laughing and panting. 'You managed!' she gasped. Which was more than another young lady was going to be able to say in that same green hollow a good few years later on.

Those big soft craters punctuate the Atlantic seaboard like giant dimples in a swathe of seersucker. Aeons ago vast storms spooned out the sand and piled it elsewhere at their whim and left it to the marram roots to bind the huge heaps into sand dunes which, in turn, turned fortress against further attacks by the wind from the west. Perhaps it was the same great holocaust that buried Stone Age Skara Brae that wrought its pattern on our shoreline too, and maybe swept away a civilization instead of petrifying it for subsequent revelation as it did in Orkney. In the lea of the dunes the seabirds and the gentler winds duly seeded the hollows and quilted them with burdock and bluebell and heliotrope, and the shimmering yellow dandelions which gave Molly her inspiration that day on the machair.

She was a great teller of tales, and even now it is to her that I most frequently turn if I need to be refreshed on some area of local lore or legend. Which is not surprising because she is descended from a long line of poets and songmakers. I didn't know that then, nor did it cross my infant mind to wonder how she – an incomer like myself – knew that, long ago, an army of warriors from a foreign land had come ashore on the beach and had set about plundering and pillaging the land as they had done up and down the whole of the rest of our coast. But here, in this very hollow, they had come face to face with a host of little people – fairies who, instead of fighting the foreigners, made them welcome and made them sit down and rest and eat and drink their fairy food. And as the fierce Norsemen nibbled the tid-bits their tiredness and their fierceness left them, and they began to hear the most beautiful music that they had ever heard in their lives and they began to dream dreams of unsurpassed beauty. One by one the warriors fell asleep and when the last of them had nodded off the fairies pulled them down into their own world on top of which we were sitting now. It was a world of music and milk and honey and the wild men had liked it so much that they never came back from it again, and never again troubled the people of Harris.

'Here! You taste this and you'll be able to go down and see them for yourself.'

I hadn't the faintest desire to consort with fairies even in their connotation of those days, but so persuasive was Molly that I couldn't refuse to taste the dandelion leaf she offered me.

It was disappointing. Not fragrant on the palate like the young primroses we used to pick at, nor honey sweet like *bainne nan gamhna* whose trumpet-shaped pistils my father had taught me to suck with dire warnings (now forgotten) not to put any plant whatsoever in my mouth without checking on its edibility with my mother or himself. Compared with those the dandelion leaves were tasteless for the first half dozen or so, and then they began to develop a tartness on the tongue which was not at all unpleasant to the child whose palate had not yet been tuned to artificial sweetness. I admitted to Molly that they 'weren't bad' (reasonable praise in Gaelic) and thus encouraged she continued to ply me with more and more and more. I didn't notice the self-satisfied smirk on her face, nor that she was being singularly abstemious herself. The promise of the trip to fairyland was forgotten for a while, and when I remembered Molly taunted me with my

35

ignorance and pointed out that I hadn't got on to the yellow petals yet.

I have no idea how many dandelions – stamens, pistils, sepals, the lot – I had consumed when Molly sprang to her feet and announced that she was going home, and off she went like a roe-deer through the marram. Nor have I any idea how long I sat and whimpered and called after her, although old experience should have told me that that was in vain, before I staggered to my feet and set off after her.

Often, in the unrestorable years of the 'local', I have fumbled home by way of quagmire and lamppost and the rest, but rarely with more difficulty than that day. The bent stroked my legs where it had whipped them before, and a great sleepiness kept pulling at my consciousness. My stomach managed to stay in place till I reached the front door behind which I could hear the blurred voices of the two mothers interrogating Molly as to where she had left me this time. The shrillness of the voices suggested that Molly's mother was both alarmed and angry and, in a woman of her calibre, the combination can be pretty fearsome. My own mother was more timid by nature, and the fact that she was on the offensive against another woman's child was proof that her anxiety – which was never far from the surface in the earlier years of her motherhood – was being fanned by intimations of disaster. I don't know whether, through the hullabaloo, she heard me scrabbling at the door, or if she suddenly decided to set out on one of her habitual forays in search of me. In any case she plucked the front door open at the precise moment at which my innards capitulated and cascaded a pool of luteous bile over the doorstep and her feet. And into it, I collapsed!

It required little medical or botanical skill to diagnose my problem. Even the robust digestive system of a Hebridean infant doesn't cope all that readily with a couple of dozen dandelions, and, as the concern for my safety took a dramatic upward turn, so the hapless Molly found the charge against her being upgraded from one of child neglect to one of homicide either culpable or attempted. Because, in the fabular pharmacopoeia in our small corner, dandelions were reckoned to be deadly poisonous!

Dandelions are not, of course, lethal or there wouldn't be any wealthy herbalists left at large. But their various constituents are individually emetic, diuretic or soporific, depending on how, and in what proportions, they are prescribed. Administered in the haphazard and frenzied way in which they had been force-fed to me they produced all the known responses at the same time and a few more for good measure.

Once they got over their initial fright the two mothers swung into galvanic action, with a firm aside to Molly to the effect that she would be attended to when they had finished with me. The one pummelled me to keep me awake while the other plied me with cups of warm salt water which I dutifully swallowed and then, in due course, rejected – each ejection becoming gratifying less bilious. At long last they must have come to the conclusion that I would survive, and as I was allowed to slip into a deep sleep I was hazily aware that my mother was removing my trousers while her mother was removing Molly's knickers for totally different reasons. If perchance I fell asleep with a smile on my face it must have been at the thought that Molly wouldn't be able to sit comfortably for a while because her mother had the muscular arms of the Harriswoman who has waulked innumerable tweeds.

When I woke up my father was back home and was being tartly complimented on once again managing to be absent when there was a crisis in the home – that most recurrent of themes in the unfinished symphony of marital disaccord, in which, paradoxically, there is nothing more infuriating than the failure of one partner (invariably the male) to rise to either taunt or insult. My father was a man of infinite patience. He was deeply in love with my mother in a fraternity where that emotion, once promulgated, was neither flaunted nor flouted. But I suspect that the maturity which had ripened in the trenches, coupled with a decade

37

of seniority, made it sometimes appear to her as if he were treating her crises as her imaginings. Which they frequently were, because, in her early years, she could find a worry in a blessing. 'I could sometimes smash that pipe of his to bitlets', I once heard her confess to a neighbour, referring to my father's habit of venting his argument on the stem of his 'Lovat' while appearing to smile into the middle distance with his eyes. I still feel that 'There's no use talking to you', isn't the real end of an argument unless it's accompanied by a clattering of plates . . .

'So you've been eating the fairies, boy!' That was enough to snap me out of the remains of my torpor.

'Down in one of the hollows at the Blue Skerry, eh? Well, well.' I waited while he examined the stem of his pipe for a crack, and tamped it and got it going again.

Long ago, apparently, the machair of Harris had no people as we know them now. Instead, the land was inhabited by 'the little folks' or the fairies and they lived a life of love and laughter and the sun always shone. The merest whiff of rain was miracled by the sun into a rainbow, and out of the rainbow the little folk spun threads of many colours for their clothes. It was a gay and carefree world until there came along men in boots, with their heads so high from the ground that they didn't even notice the earth upon which they were stamping nor the life they were trampling underfoot. So the fairies went underground – all of them except the ones who couldn't face a life without the sun, and who stayed above and turned themselves into flowers, the proudest of which was the Notched Flower of St Bridget as the dandelion is called in Gaelic. High up above it all, the sun watched what was happening with sorrow. Where it had twinkled down on the earth all day long before, it now took to closing its eyes at night, and, in sympathy, the dandelion took to closing and opening its eyes with it, so that, to this day, even when the clouds are hiding the sun you can tell its rising and its setting by watching the Flower of St Bridget!

'I hope the new house is coming along as well as the stories are doing!'

I could tell by the twinkle in my mother's voice that her tension had vanished, and the relief of it closed the file on the Dandelion in my mind.

It was to be many years later, when a furious sand-storm laid bare Stone Age coffins and skeletons in that same hollow by the Blue Skerry, that it dawned on me that there had been a subtle thread common to the two folk legends that Molly and my father, in their very different ways, had brought to life for me that day.

'The house is coming along fine,' said my father as he put his pipe in his pocket and went to the table. 'I was burning a few sticks to test the chimney just before I came home. We must be thinking of ordering a grate soon.' He rubbed his eyes quickly with his knuckles and yawned – the token gesture to the Almighty to which he had reduced the traditional grace before meat – and began to eat, little knowing that in those casual few sentences about the chimney he had laid the foundations of the one and only phobia which was to obsess him for the rest of his life.

Chapter Five

I have no diaries to consult. No letters. None of the tools of the trade of the historian or the hagiographer of which I am neither anyway. Nor have I the awesome memory of my old friend, the late Sir Compton MacKenzie who – in his mid eighties – used to regale me with recollections of the Victorian scene as viewed from his perambulator. Far less have I the self-confident talent of a revered uncle of mine who, in the face of the unimpeachable evidence of no less expert a witness than his own mother and my devout grandmother, would graphically recall not only the looks but the conversations and peccadillos of people who were dead long before he was born.

All I have are the milestones of childhood – occasions, mishaps and moments which were momentous of their time and in their place – that have remained only because, at the beginning of each new day, they seemed to be promising a great adventure which, in the end, turned out to be just another life. Such a milestone was the Day of the Dandelions, and it's only because I remember *it* that I'm now able to remember the day which followed it.

The evening of the Day of the Dandelions had passed sullenly, and even our regular visitor didn't arrive to break the monotony. Wee Barabel, as she was called, lived on her own in a tumbledown thatched cottage on the edge of the moor. Like all the others who lived there she was a relic of the old population who had survived the several evictions and population shifts, but unlike Great Aunt

Rachel, she did not have the self-confidence of a long pedigree and an education. In fact she was a simple old soul who, under today's social conditions and observances, would have been taken into care of some sort or other, because she lived in her one little room in conditions of squalor even for those times. She claimed that she had no idea how old she was, but she must have convinced somebody at some stage or other that she had enough years to merit the weekly pension for which she thanked 'Loy George and the Lord' in that order in the garbled prayers into which she was liable to launch at the drop of a hat and in totally unpredictable circumstances. Despite her occasionally embarrassing outbursts of devotion she had the reputation of being a witch, but that did not deter the few teenage lumps of boys who lived in her vicinity from teasing her mercilessly although, secretly, they were scared of her and wouldn't dare offend her openly. The older people were sorry for her and made sure that she never lacked for milk or fuel, and though they might inwardly groan when they saw her appearing, the womenfolk always reached for the kettle and plied her with tea and scones when she arrived.

My father was very fond of Wee Barabel because she was full of stories of life in the olden days. She would retail – with what accuracy I know not – lurid accounts of soldiers coming round and clearing people out of their homes at the landlords' behest to make room for the expansion of their farms, and of rapacious factors ploughing up graveyards to plant potatoes. My subsequent study of local history makes me suspect that Barabel's narratives were concocted from the legends of several preceding generations, but, like Great Aunt Rachel's sagas, they always had elements of the truth in them. My father was an addict of old folks' tales and, even when he had heard a story countless times before, had the wonderful art of appearing to be engrossed in whatever was being told him while his mind was miles away concentrating on some much more mundane problem of his own. He was the

41

perfect captive audience for Wee Barabel whom he had known from his boyhood visits to Aunt Rachel. And so, from the very first day that we ensconced ourselves in the schoolhouse she would totter down the hill sharp on the dot of eight o'clock, which she regarded as seven o'clock because, like many of the older folk on the hill, she absolutely refused to acknowledge British Summer Time and adhered to what she called 'God's Time'. Her punctuality was nothing short of miraculous because she had never in her life allowed a clock in her house on the grounds that she didn't want to hear her life ticking away. But for once Wee Barabel didn't appear. And all evening my father fidgeted and worried about her, thus totally cancelling out my mother's thinly veiled relief at the prospect of an evening of privacy during which she might pin my father down to discussing matters of fairly pressing importance like, for example, the furnishing of the new house. Long after I had been unceremoniously hustled off to bed I could hear, through the wall, strictures like 'Your son's been at death's door and all you can do is worry about Wee Barabel', and 'If you spent more evenings working on the new house rather than listening to the maunderings of Barabel we might be in a place of our own by winter.' The themes of marital disharmony vary little with successive generations!

Father was very subdued over breakfast, and as soon as it was over he got up from the table and announced that he was going up the hill to see if Barabel was all right. My mother, whose conscience had obviously begun to prick her during the night, agreed that he should. I seized my chance to ask if I might go along to the new house to await his arrival there, and to my slight astonishment my mother agreed – with dire warnings to keep to the side of the road and watch out for cars!

I set off, and to my joy I found myself teaming up with Gillespie, an incomer boy four days younger than myself with whom I had barely made passing acquaintance till then. Gillespie and I were to become partners in many scrapes in the years ahead but, that day, we were still at the stage of warily weighing each other up. He could hardly believe that I had been given permission to explore the new house on my own and we raced each other towards it.

The new house consisted of a concrete foundation out of which sprouted a wooden skeleton of upright beams and criss-crosses of rafter with, at the south end, a stone and mortar stack from which grew a tall cast iron pipe – the chimney that my father had tested the day before. The whole thing looked good and it smelt beautifully of resinous new wood, but I doubt if it would have held our attention for long if it weren't for the fact that, inside, it was an Aladdin's cave of saws, chisels, hammers and nails – all the basic tools of the carpenter's trade which my father would have forbidden me for their safety, and my mother for mine. And there we were, all alone, and with no danger of being interrupted because I knew that once my father reached Barabel's place it would take him a long time to disentangle himself from her yarning while making excuses to avoid partaking of her dubiously hygienic tea. Nobody else was liable to disturb Gillespie and myself. Or so we thought. But, unbeknownst to us, and fortunately for us, there was, plodding towards the village, one of humbler minions of the Board of Agriculture in the shape of the Stallion Man.

The larger and much longer established village next to ours boasted a sizeable stud of plough horses which consisted of a motley assortment of mares and geldings. The latter were not of much use to the former, so the Board had undertaken as one of its duties the provision, once a year, of a stallion to service the mares who conveniently appeared to develop the same desires within the space of the same fortnight. And the Board also provided a little man to service the stallion.

I have never got round to discovering whether the stallion was a highly prized and pedigreed native of Arabia who had disgraced himself with Lord Rosebery or the Aga Khan, or just the bye-blow of some coal haulage company who had escaped the knife. I suspect the former, because he was tall and proud and expected to be waited upon hand and foot and everything else. His attendant wasn't allowed to ride him nor even to place his luggage on his back, and I can recall few more pathetic sights than a five-foot man in an old tweed suit, with a portmanteau in one hand and the bridle of a sixteen-hand stallion in the other, trudging the sweaty Harris miles on a hot summer's day. At least the stallion could look forward to something for which his energies were being conserved. At the end of the day the man would have neither energy nor prospect.

From infancy onwards, we crofter children grew up surrounded by quadrupedal sex and it is a miracle of instinct that we didn't accept quadrupedal modes as the norm instead of having to await enlightenment from *Playboy* and the *Kama Sutra*. We had seen the bull and the ram, the dog and the cat, set about their business purposefully after minimal skirmishing. But our aristocratic stallion – and for all I know this may be an effetism of aristocracy at all levels – had to be helped. After a bit of sniffing and snorting around an impatient mare, the stallion would wait for the man to take him by one of the front fetlocks and encourage him upwards. Only then would the animal languidly release from his body something which, for all the world, resembled the black concertina hose which comes out of the back of a modern tumble-drier, and this the stallion man had to guide into the appropriate channel. It can't have been the most enlightening of professional duties although veterinary surgeons have to do worse, but it didn't deserve the opprobrium which accrued to the poor Stallion Man. He was the object of jibes and innuendous jokes to his face and behind his back, and, to this day there is no greater Gaelic insult to hurl at a toady or someone who performs another's menial jobs than to call him a 'cock boy'. But that year's cock boy

44

was to gain for himself a moment of glory, and a dinner before which, for once, he wasn't made to wash his hands.

Gillespie and I had had a hey-day, sawing and drilling and nailing together pieces of wood into models of our imaginings, and we had begun to tire of the whole thing while we still had ten fingers apiece. Just as we were thinking of trailing off in search of some other adventure I spotted the box of matches which my father had forgetfully left on the new hearth. And his comments about having tested the chimney flashed back to me. It was obvious from the charred remains of shavings at the base of the chimney pipe that they were the very stuff that he had used, and there were still mounds of them around. Between us, it took only a few minutes to make a sizeable heap and, after several broken matches, we had it ablaze. Had we left it at that things mightn't have got out of hand, but our triumph went to our heads when we looked up and saw, spiralling from the chimney top, shapely puffs of creamy white smoke that would have sealed the election of half a hundred Popes. We decided to compound our success by heaping on to the burning shavings all the constructions that we had nailed together during the previous hour, and soon we had a roaring bonfire that would have roasted an ox – and might conceivably have roasted us had the Stallion Man not arrived at the gate as the wooden frame-work of the gable-end began to catch fire.

It must have been the first time that the Stallion Man moved quickly in his life. He whipped the huge felt horse cloth off the horse's back, rushed into the house, threw us out bodily and unceremoniously, and, like a man possessed, began to smother the flames. The situation was under control by the time my father arrived on the scene, gasping for breath and ashen faced, after a burst across the hill from Barabel's such as he had probably not indulged in since he had gone over the top at the Battle of Arras.

'Thank God you're all right', he said, looking at Gillespie and myself. 'And as for you', he went on turning to the

Stallion Man, 'it was Fate that sent you the way.'

The Stallion Man appeared not to hear him.

'This is as tattered as a whore's hole', he grumbled, thrusting his raw, scorched fist through the middle of the singed horse cloth, and I noticed the muscle in my father's jaw twitch as his eyes flicked in the direction of Gillespie and myself. 'The Board's going to have something to say about this!'

He was wrong. By the time he left the schoolhouse, cleaned and salved and with a good meal in him, the stallion's broad back was draped in a folded suit-length of Harris Tweed which had been ordered for Sir Thomas Lipton who was an occasional visitor to Harris on one or other of his yachts. As it turned out, the ripening years wouldn't have allowed Sir Thomas much wear out of the tweed anyway, but when the cock boy came round the island next he was sporting a suit that would have graced a game-keeper while the stallion seemed perfectly happy in a traditional horse cloth with the Government's seal still crisp on it.

I don't know what quiet persuasion my father had used on my mother but, apart from the first flurry of nervous anxiety, she never referred to the near catastrophe again. Father mentioned it once during the evening. While my mother was putting the baby to bed he looked at me for a long time over the bowl of his pipe, which he had a habit of tilting ceiling-wards when he was in quizzical mood, and then said, 'I don't believe in giving rows for things which won't happen again anyway, but I'd give a lot to know what you'll be up to next.' Obviously I was in no position to hazard a guess myself, but before the silence became embarrassing my mother came through from the bedroom having remembered that she hadn't heard what had befallen Wee Barabel who had been tangentially involved in it all.

Apparently the whole problem had been there for my father to see and to solve as soon as he reached her little hovel. On the night before last a couple of the hillside lads

– 'the bloods' as they were called – had crept up while she was asleep and stuffed her one and only window with turf. And she had spent thirty-six hours in bed waiting for the dawn, puzzled only by the fact that her bladder was making her reach for the pot more often than usual. It was while he was letting in the light and trying to comfort Barabel for the lost day in her life that father had noticed the smoke and flames rising from the roadside down below.

'Boys!' said my mother, as she was to say so often in the future, 'I'm afraid it's worse they get as they get older.' And that reminded her that it was time for me to be in bed. I was conscious of the fact that she was even more solicitous than usual as she tucked me into bed, whispering so as not to waken the baby.

'You close your eyes and go to sleep now; you've had quite a day of it!' She kissed me and crossed over to close the curtains against the light of the setting sun.

'Look mammy', I said, sitting up and holding up the old woollen bedspread which had come down through a couple of generations, 'this coverlet is as tattered as a whore's hole.'

She jerked as if someone had hit her in the rib-cage. Her mouth opened, but she decided to say nothing. And she walked quickly from the bedroom leaving the curtains half drawn. I lay back on the pillow confirmed in my suspicion that I had found a new phrase worth hoarding for future use.

Chapter Six

My father went through the whole of that portion of his life in which I shared, with a mortal fear of fire. In all the years of my boyhood nothing would persuade him to go to bed before every other member of the family had retired, and when the lean years came and my mother would sometimes have to sit up late into the night spinning, he would sit up with her, reading or just puffing at his pipe. And often, during the night, I remember half wakening as he padded through to the living room to check yet again that the last embers were ashing, even although he had raked and doubled raked them before going to bed in the first place. Heaven knows he was a late bedder at the best of times, but though he fervently maintained a theory that a man's sleeping pattern is governed by the state of the tide at the moment of his birth, I suspect that the tidal influences – in the theory of which, incidentally, I firmly believe – were, in his case, heightened by the more mundane effects of the scorch inflicted on his persona by the efforts of Gillespie and myself.

The near-destruction of the house before it had been built was, paradoxically, responsible for it being completed on schedule when it had been limping along before. My father, swallowing his pride, got up early the next morning and set off to walk the sixteen miles north, whence we had come those many months before, to solicit the help of my mother's cousin, who was a carpenter to trade and a shepherd at heart, and had the good nature that one would expect in one embodying such hallowed characteristics. He jumped at the chance of spending a week in highly prized sheep country and, in a couple of days he arrived with a year-old ewe as a contribution to my father's flock, and a box containing a neatly arrayed outfit of carpentry tools which I was allowed to admire only from afar. Each day he worked from eight o'clock till six – all the while discoursing on sheep through endless mouthfuls of nails – and, in the evenings, he tramped the machair and the moorland sizing up the crofters' sheep and lambs as if he were contemplating buying them. Which is probably how he dreamt. Although he was a fortunate man with a trade, the myth of the freedom of the land was in his essence. He lived in the cheek-by-jowl environment of a harbour village – a town by our standards – and he could only indulge his fancy by grazing a few sheep on the rough hill above Tarbert. To him our green acres must have been the Canaan of his imaginings, and his gift of a young ewe, although generous beyond measure, was also, probably, an unconscious sacrifice to the undefinable 'might-have-been' which puts a slight check in the smile of most of us as we look across our own boundary walls.

Within a week the new house was finished. Its corrugated iron walls gleamed a blue grey; the roof was a bright red, and the windows white; it consisted of two rooms, each twelve feet square with a door leading straight from the living room to the bedroom. There had been some corrugated iron left over, so a small porch had been added at the front to take the bite out of the west winds which would blow square on from the Atlantic. The porch was a luxury, because the grand design was that the house would serve as a home for a year or two till a roomy stone house would be built, subsidized by the Board of Agriculture, and the original building would become the byre. That was the pattern which had been established in places like Skye and the mainland where the crofters had won their land long before us, and that same pattern was now beginning to be seen to establish itself in Harris.

For some reason or other I have no recollection of moving in although the day must have been a very important one in my parents' lives. Vaguely, I remember a hurried slapping of wall-paper, a table and four chairs arriving from somewhere, a tall press into which were unpacked boxes of crockery – some items of which were greeted as half-forgotten wedding presents from Aunt Catherine, from Uncle Alex and the rest. Beside the press and conveniently placed for the door stood an old fashioned wash-hand basin and ewer table which had been adapted to hold two large pails which, as I was to discover very quickly, had to be kept permanently filled with water from the river which ran behind and round the house. The south, gable-end of the room was dominated almost entirely by a massive black iron stove decorated with a stainless steel fluted border round the top edge – an adornment which, I concluded fairly early on, had been put there for the sole purpose of making the black-leading of the monster even more of a Saturday night chore than the ritual polishing of the family boots. Of its time it must have been very advanced in design, and geared for the house-wife working without the advantages of any form of interior plumbing. On top it could keep two pots boiling and four simmering, while the central fire heated a large, efficient oven at one end and a capacious water boiler at the other. Along its front the whole contraption was heavily embossed with its trade name which proclaimed it to be, for some reason best known to the makers, a 'Modern Mistress'. I haven't seen its counterpart for many a year, but I'm reminded of it from time to time when some local Highland newspaper or other carries an advertisement from an antique dealer looking for one. The text can range from the vulgar to the lewd depending on the urgency with which the would-be purchaser attempts to underline his quest, and the state of repair which he is willing to accept.

The pride of my father's life was the ancient tall-backed five-seater bench which ran below the window at right angles to the stove, and took up every inch of the front wall right up to the back of the living room door. It was useful in that it sat five or even six people, albeit in circumstances that were conducive neither to comfort nor conversation, and because it could serve as a rather spartan spare bed for visitors who weren't kith or kin enough to treble up with my brother and myself in the second double bed in the bedroom. It looked exactly like what it was – an oaken church pew which, according to my father, had been the family seat of the Clan MacLeod in the ancient Church of St Clement's in Rodel. St Clement's, notable as the only cruciform church in the Outer Hebrides, had last been renovated by Lord Dunmore in 1840, or thereabouts, and I was never able to discover where, or how, the pew had weathered the intervening hunk of century. Its alleged antiquity earned for it, in my father's mind, the sort of mystic reverence that many English people accord to the Coronation Chair of Edward I, and rather fewer to the Coronation Stone at Kingston-upon-Thames. But the more eloquent he waxed about its religious antecedents the less comfortable my more superstitious mother felt with it as a piece of domestic furniture, and she found it hard to summon up enough imagination to make it more accept-able just because it had been hallowed or otherwise by successive generations of her own Chief's bottoms. As time went on, however, and no strange lights, or appari-tions or rattlings of ancient bones manifested themselves, I suspect that she began to doubt its authenticity and thus managed to live with it as she lived with so many of my father's more romantic notions.

I suspect that he himself would have queried the suggestion of a romantic streak in his nature and arrogated to himself, rather, a sense of history. But the dividing line between the two can be strangely blurred during times of scrabble for survival such as the early years undoubtedly were for some of the new villagers, and certainly for my parents. I am sure, for example, that my mother, who had come out of a fairly comfortable parental home, must have wished that she had more money with which to furnish the new house instead of having to make do with ecclesiastical discards of questionable aestheticism and unquestionable discomfort, and so, inescapably ecclesiastical as the connections might still be, her optimism must have been kittled by the news of the Manse roup – an event of such rare occurrence nowadays, as then, that it may require a bit of scene setting even for Scottish readers. . . .

Today there still stands, high above the village, a superb Georgian building which is haunted from time to time by such unethereal spirits as Derek Cooper and the man from Egon Ronay searching, in the public interest, for rarefied qualities of bodily and spirituous comfort. It was built, around the middle of the eighteenth century as the residence for the local minister who was, at that time, appointed and retained by the local landlord and was, consequently, divided in his loyalty between his Lord and his master in much the same way as the clerics of the unreformed Church in England have now to balance their allegiance discreetly between the Monarch and the Almighty. The manses were built large so that their incumbents could, in their off-duty times, act as hosts to the hordes of visitors who were then beginning to descend on the Highlands in the slip-stream of Queen Victoria, and whose blood or station entitled them to hospitality one degree lower than that of whichever belted earl happened to be the landowner at the time. With the Disruption, however, the Church in Scotland largely cast off the shackles of patronage, and big manses such as ours were freed from the influence of the estate and left to be the private homes of ministers who – no matter how formidable their virility – could not afford families large enough to fill the honeycombs of bedchambers, any more than they could afford to offer hospitality to the overflow guests from the 'Big House'.

The venerable gentleman who was minister of South

Harris at the time of our arrival there had, late in life, married, most improbably, a French woman many years his junior – which had probably no bearing on the fact that he died very suddenly round about the time that we moved into the new house. And shortly afterwards it was announced that the contents of the manse would be sold off by public roup or auction. In those days it would have been a very intrepid dealer indeed who would have ventured to the Outer Hebrides on the strength of one single domestic auction sale, and my mother must have had a shrewd idea that a few items of suitable furniture would be going at bargain rates – certainly something in the way of small easy chairs to add a modicum of comfort to the tiny area of living room that was left available to her by the pew from St Clements.

It would be ridiculous to pretend that I remember the briefing she gave my father as she rummaged in the trinkets compartment of the big red chest which had been pressed into service as a sitting place at the end of the table. But I do remember that the money with which she emerged was the sum total of what she had set aside for the purchase, in due course, of congoleum which was the very latest in floor covering of the period and considered to be very much more 'in the fashion' than the traditional wax-cloth. Nor do I more than suspect that it was after some considerable heart-searching that she had made up her mind to forgo the coveted congoleum in favour of possibly unrepeatable bargains of furniture. In fact I would probably have forgotten the whole evening long ere this were it not that there was something incongruous, which couldn't fail to imprint itself on my mind, in the picture of my father setting off for the manse with a wheelbarrow and wearing his Sunday suit.

It may have been, of course, my mother who stamped the evening on my mind. It is difficult now to disentangle her subsequent good-humoured recountings of the event from the actuality, but it's highly probable that she spent the long hours of waiting describing to me the arm-chairs which she had remembered seeing on one of her few visits to the servants' quarters of the manse. And methinks there was mention of a rocking chair. And may be she kept me amused by telling me where each item might go, and which of the present items would have to be moved and where. The evening would certainly be long, because anything which savoured of social intercourse – be it sheep fank or prayer meeting – was liable to be protracted in a community in which the population was scattered, and new to each other, and with few excuses for meeting socially in more than ones or twos. It's strange how long a new populace, artificially planted, takes to develop the rhythms of a society; we were too new even for funerals.

There must still have been some lingering daylight when my father returned because long before he reached the gate I could see that, if he had bought anything at all, it was of such small dimensions that it didn't show above the sides of the wheelbarrow. When I drew mother's attention to this she merely shrugged in the resigned way that she was already beginning to adopt and said something to the effect that the prices must have been too high.

But her guess was wrong. And her resignation vanished when my father appeared with a slightly guilty smile on his face and carrying in his arms a bundle of trophies from the roup. It consisted of two ancient dinner plates of the kind that one hangs on the wall with wire and hopes, usually in vain, that some future generation will redeem them for their antique value, and a large bundle of books which included Gibbon's *Decline and Fall of the Roman Empire*, *The Lays of Ancient Rome* by Thomas Babington Macaulay (with whom Great Aunt Rachel claimed acquaintance) and some obscure volumes on the language and literature of the Scottish Highlands. Before he realized that his popularity was not exactly at its zenith he let slip that he had bid for a fiddle which, mercifully for him, he had failed to get. For sure my mother's friendliest remark of that evening was that the house would be the envy of the neighbours when she carpeted the floor with *The Lays of Ancient Rome* with *The Decline and Fall* for underfelt! But the fact remains that one unimpressive-looking volume out of that night's bundle has, by chance more than by design, followed me through the years, and if I were to take it from my book-shelves and sell it now it would cover the house in Wilton carpeting from wall to wall – let alone congoleum. And as for *The Lays of Ancient Rome*, I owed to them more than a little of whatever facility I came to acquire in the English language in my early years.

The congoleum, however, would have made a big difference to my life as well as to my mother's. Even today, when it's usual to have gravel paths or pavings round houses, when there are modern floor coverings and carpets by the acre everywhere, and when there is a whole science of gadgetry for lightening cleaning, keeping a country cottage floor clean can be one of the minor irritants of life. It was more than a minor irritant then.

One of the many things which we never achieved was a path from the main road to the house, and even had we done so, all our outdoor work was concentrated in fields which – whatever the golden memories of childhood may suggest – got their fair share of the rain which falls generously in the Western Isles. Consequently, no matter how diligently one scraped one's boots or bare feet, as the case might be, the 'keeping respectable' of the floor was not only an irritant but a problem. And it was a problem in which I had to share.

For as long as I can remember my mother was determined that if any of her sons should ever find himself 'widowed or worse' (whatever that might mean) he should be able to look after himself and his house, and, from the earliest days that I can remember in a home of our own I had to do my share of the house-work, come what may. In due course the chores were to be extended to include making and mending and cookery – for all of which I have subsequently been grateful – but in the beginning, even before I went to school, the clearly defined areas of my responsibility were the water pails, of which two had to be filled night and morning and four on a Saturday night; the polishing of the range (as the 'Modern Mistress' was called for short); the constant replenishment of the peat bucket from the pile at the end of the house; and the provision of *mealtrach* and fine shell sand for the cleaning of the floor.

I have never had occasion to find out what the English for *mealtrach* is, and it's not worth my while finding out now since I am unlikely ever to have to use the word or the substance again. It is, in fact, the very fine roots of the marram grass which mat loosely together and fringe the under edges of the wind-blown sand cliffs of the sea shore like pubic hair peeping out from an incautious bathing costume. Every Saturday in life, till blessed linoleum came along, I had to forage along the sea cliffs and collect a sackful of *mealtrach* and carry it home, and then, from the same source, ferry innumerable pails of fine white sand. Then, on the Saturday evening, my mother would scrub the wooden floor with carbolic soap, using the *mealtrach* as a scourer, and before the floor was dry she would cover it liberally with sand. Just before bedtime she would brush off the sand, leaving the wooden flooring pristine white for the Sabbath. Woe betide the person who left nature's last call to 'the pee-tub' unanswered till after the sand had been swept!

During the period of settling into the new house I had lost touch with my erstwhile sparring partner, Molly, whose family must have moved out of the schoolhouse and into their new house about the same time as we moved ourselves. It was a friendship that was destined not to last anyway because a couple of years' difference in age is a life-time in a boy and girl relationship at that stage but, as so often happens, they are the childish scrapes into which we got together that have cemented a friendship in life much later on. When we meet now on what was once home territory for us both, and still is for her, the conversation invariably includes reference to some trifling incident that was important of its time, and which the one recollects and the other pretends to remember.

The reverse was the situation with Gillespie. A life-time and, literally, the depth of the world have separated us almost certainly forever, but as we grew up and the village grew up around us we were closer than many brothers. We weren't encouraged to see much of each other for a few weeks after our escapade with the matches, and I suspect that the one mother was, in the nature of things, inclined to blame the other mother's son. But we teamed up again when it turned out that *mealtrach* collection was one of his mandatory duties too, and the companionship made the chore into more of an adventure. And then, as August wore on, a whole new world was opened up to us as we began to accompany our mothers when they went crotal scraping.

Moors can still stir deep hidden, primeval, fears in the most sophisticated of people, and the very adjectives that are most frequently used to describe them, like 'bleak' and 'empty' are evocative of aloneness and remoteness from help should help be required. Our moor was vast, and I never felt afraid on it except once in sudden fog, but our women would never venture far on to it except in couples when they had to, which was only really at crotal gathering time. But they were, of course, the last generation to emerge from the thrall of superstition which is part of the warp and woof of the traditional fabric of primitive country life everywhere before education rips it apart for better or for worse. It was only in my father's boyhood that the various Compulsory Education Acts began to be enforced, but it was to be a long time before reading and its various allied leisure pastimes began to supplant the dark night story sessions about creatures like the 'Water Horse' who could emerge from moorland tarns and, briefly assuming handsome human form, would capture and carry off into the depths unwary young women wandering the moors for some purpose like the collecting of crotal! It takes a long time to expunge deep-rooted traditions from the sub-conscious and, unfortunately, they're the best traditions that tend to go first.

Crotal is a brittle grey lichen that grows slowly on undisturbed rocks and ancient walls. When it is 'ripe' it begins to lift off the parent surface and, at that stage, it becomes what has been for centuries the most popular agent for the dyeing of wool for tweed, and, for the last hundred years or so especially Harris Tweed.

Every colour imaginable could be obtained from a common vegetable source, and the tweeds from particular districts could be fairly accurately identified from the proliferation of plants native to these parts. In our area, which had been the heartland of the Harris Tweed industry when it became formally established as a craft, there was a wealth of colour to be distilled from nature because of the lush growth on machair and on moor. And every girl, up to my mother's generation at least, had to know exactly which colour each plant provided when it was boiled with a fleece. For example crotal itself gave a rich reddish brown; groundsel gave a bitter lemon; rib-wort gave blue; water-lily, black; heather tips, pastel green; willow leaves, soft yellow. And so on. Even the peat soot from the chimney gave a beautiful cinnamon colour. And when each individual ingredient was boiled with the wool the addition to the brew of a handful of sorrel ensured that the colour remained fast forever more. The list of colours and their blendings was endless. But the most popular of them all was crotal, except among sailors who would never wear it because they maintained that crotal always returned to the rocks.

The only implement required for scraping the crotal was an old soup spoon with one side diagonally sliced off so as to leave a sharp tip to reach into crevices; and it was armed with a soup spoon and a sack and a pack of oatmeal scones and milk or whey that Gillespie's mother and mine set off on their expeditions into the moor to build up their stocks of lichen against the late summer, by which time the sheep would be sheared and the fleeces cleaned and ready for dyeing in the aged three-legged pots which were as essential an item of equipment as the pee-tub itself.

Because crotal was such a popular item in the dyeing process the nearer rocks had been scraped clean by successive generations of the old population, and because the lichen took years to regenerate itself our mothers had to press further and further into the moorland to find rocks that hadn't already been denuded. Gillespie and I were howled down for sacrilege when we suggested, as we thought helpfully and logically, that the whole operation could be completed easily and expeditiously in one quick sortie to the old graveyard where the tombstones of the past were coated with enough crisp rich crotal to dye flocks of sheep. Apparently not only the spirits of the long since departed but the Lord in person would wreak vengeance for such desecration.

Moorland air and coastal air are as different as wine and beer, and it's on the same senses that they make their separate impressions. The breeze from the sea attacks the taste buds and the nostrils, wrenching an immediate response. But, even half way up, on the hip of a mountain, the wind has a bouquet that is light and heady at the same time and the sleep that follows a day of it is as smooth as the sleep that follows love.

Nor is the moor silent as people would have one suppose. Unless the spiralling song of a lark is silence, or the purr of a dragonfly, or the rustling of the heather in a breeze that is too light for the face to feel. No, the moor is only *comparatively* silent when there is another noise level with which to compare, and that is why the desultory distinctive scrape of the crotal spoons on the rocks has etched itself on the memory and can be recalled now in the conscious act of remembering.

Our mothers talked little as they worked. Now and again one would call out to the other that she had found 'a good rock' and her claim would be confirmed by the long peeling scratch of her spoon as she eased a blister of lichen

59

off the stone and into her sack, and that would be followed by urgent little tinkles of metal on stone as she dug into the crevices for the more reluctant morsels of crotal. 'Make sure it isn't Goat's Beard!' would come the taunt, referring to another yellowish crust that had no value as a dye and would only be mistaken for crotal by a novice or a half-wit. Ripostes that had long since lost any claim to originality were still good for a giggle when the heart was young and the mind was spare of experience beyond the paramaters of domesticity.

Gillespie and I were invariably enjoined to search for White Heather and not to come back till we had found 'an armful'. It was a dodge to keep us occupied because to every acre of Bell Heather and Common Ling there was rarely more than a modest clump of the white kind and it was as difficult as four-leafed clover to find. But there were other distractions to take over. Occasionally a vacated grouse nest. Now and then a secrecy of blaeberries which had to be plucked as gently as joy if they weren't to burst before surrendering their succulence which was tart and sweet at the same time. And everywhere – some still shoulder high to a boy – the ancient ruins of the generation of ancestors, who, two centuries before, had been the first batch of West Harris people to be evicted and shipped off to Canada but had never arrived on the other side. Of course we didn't know that then, nor would we have understood if we had been told. Even our mothers, who balked at the thought of scraping crotal off the ornamental tombstones in the kirkyard, thought nothing of scraping clean those sadder, lonelier memorials to which history had denied even the dignity of haunting.

If there were ghosts around perhaps they smiled to hear laughter coming back as the women called halt for the 'half sack break' as they called it, because the moment to stop and eat was not dictated by the hour but by the achievement of the first half full sack of crotal. And then the scones and the milk were laid out on the cloth in which they had been wrapped and the four of us would sit down to what

60

the gentry would doubtless have called a picnic. 'The best cook is hunger', according to the Gaelic proverb, although it goes limp in the translation; but the sharp appetite of the moorland has an edge of its own. And, added to it, the glow of importance that hasn't altered or diminished a whit for ever sophisticating generations of boys when mothers sit down and embrace them in talk which is neither lisped nor joked nor forced nor condescending – only warm with love, and generous of time.

But in the last of those crotal outings that I took part in, there kept intruding on my instinct a recurrent and only half understood theme of conversation, plucking at an indefinable and elusive worry. It had all to do with new trousers and new jerseys and that the days were running out and that school was about to begin. Not yet. Not tomorrow. 'But not . . .', snapped Gillespie's mother when he spilt the milk over her ' . . . not before time.'

Chapter Seven

If it is true that only those whom the Gods love die young, then Miss Dalbeith is still around somewhere . . . which is why I have given her a name other than the name by which she was christened or launched or whatever. Not that the name really matters because, whatever I call her, there are at least sixteen people who, if they read this, will know who I'm talking about – sixteen out of the seventeen who were present on the day that school began.

I remember that my father was very edgy and nervous that morning, but at first I put it down to the fact that he was probably ill at ease in his Sunday suit on a week-day. And, even in retrospect, I prefer to think that some secret thought was worrying a man who had spent five years in the trenches other than the idea of meeting Miss Dalbeith.

I myself wasn't all that relaxed. For one thing, my father insisted on holding my hand for the full five hundred yards which separated our new house from the school and I was anxious lest it get round the village that I needed moral support from a man who was six times my age. There was the memory of the veiled threats which had been made of what would happen to me if I didn't temper my transgressions when I went to school. And, above all, I couldn't help remembering how firmly my mother used to check some of the men for using certain adjectives when they were discussing the teacher in front of me. These discussions hadn't meant much to me at the time, but fragments of them were niggling at me now that I was on the point of meeting the lady face to face.

It was on the tip of my tongue to suggest to my father that we should turn back home and devote a day of autumn sunshine to painting the outside of our new house. But as I was framing the idea so that it wouldn't sound suspicious in words, the school gate creaked under my father's hand. It was a low, slow skreek . . . as if the gate, which had seen so many boys come and go in its day, was warning me – like a dog baying a warning of approaching doom. The immediate result of the rusty protest was that it brought the head of Miss Dalbeith to the window as the bell brings the waiter in a well oiled hotel. The head stayed there, between a pile of books and a vase of dejected wild flowers, and only the eyes moved behind horn-rimmed spectacles to follow us up to the blistered green door. The picture has been re-lit for me from time to time in recent years, when I have watched television close-ups of weathered female politicians at Party Conferences listening disapprovingly to speakers resisting the re-introduction of capital punishment.

To say that my father abandoned me is just stating the simple truth. He exchanged a few incomprehensible sentences in English with Miss Dalbeith as he handed me over, and, out of the corner of my eye I saw him turn on his heel and walk back to the school gate like a man with an old weight off his mind and a new one on his conscience.

At the age of five, everybody over twenty is ancient to a little boy, and so I can't say whether Miss Dalbeith was really old or not. And it is also why I can't be sure that she isn't alive and fit and well and reading this. But she was certainly an imposing woman – taller than all but one of the men in our village; and she held herself very straight because she believed that posture was the prerequisite of well-being – physical and moral – although, with hindsight, I doubt if temptation ever came her way to incline her from the upright. For my part, I was to suffer much in the months ahead from her disciplines, not least of which was spending endless hours standing in a corner of the schoolroom with a book balanced on my head as she tried to eliminate the slouch with which the Almighty has endowed my particular branch of Clan Donald for generations.

Her spectacles were so heavy that I can remember little about her face except that it was tanned a rich compost brown, and, come to think of it, so must have been the rest of her, because she was forever being stumbled across, sun-bathing in the nude in odd corners of the common grazing land, when the men were out shepherding. But despite the disparagements of the time it was later claimed that our sheep were never so well tended as they were in the summers of Miss Dalbeith.

Like a lot of people I still have a slight horror of walking into a crowded hall, and, for me, I think it started that moment when my father deserted me inside that schoolroom door. Sixteen pairs of eyes seemed to be tearing me apart as if they were trying to recognize a stranger inside the new Harris Tweed suit which my mother had finished making for me just the night before, and when I attempted to twitch a cheery little smile there was no flicker of recognition from the boisterous boys and girls – some of whom I had been playing with yesterday. When I was beginning to wonder what had transformed them all into a crowd of zombies, I was given my first clue. There was a bellow from behind me, followed quickly by a vicious tug of my left ear and I was spun round to stare into the knees of Miss Dalbeith's hand-knitted stockings. I didn't have time to ponder that I had never seen a strange woman's knees before, or that Miss Dalbeith was ahead of the fashion charts, because a scalping tug of my fore-lock and another stream of English incomprehensibility took my head back and my face up to meet her spectacles. What did dawn on me was that Miss Dalbeith and I were going to have some difficulty understanding each other, because, while I had enough Gaelic to last me for the rest of my life, she didn't have a word of Gaelic in her head.

I would willingly have solved the language problem for her by slipping off home – but she was a resourceful woman. She led me by the forelock to the end of a five-seater desk where there was an empty seat beside a girl. She patted the wooden seat first, and then mine. She said 'sit' and pressed me down hard, and so I learnt my first word of English as if I were being groomed for Crufts. From a slot in the front of the desk she extracted a wooden framed slate which she presented to me along with a thin slate pencil and she signalled that I should occupy myself in silence while she proceeded to harangue Primary Five which consisted of one boy called George. I had always envied George his skill in shinning up the telegraph poles which were beginning to sprout in our village. Now I envied him his apparent mastery of the English language.

The schoolroom was square and high and green and yellow. On one wall there was a huge faded parchment map with vast areas of red on it which I learnt in time to be the British Empire. There was a variety of jaded posters, only one of which I remember because of its manifest absurdity. It showed scantily clad, floppily bosomed women up to their knees in water cutting corn, and it didn't take much education to recognize that it was fake. Putting aside the artist's eye for colour completely, I knew that our women would rather die than be seen in that state of *déshabille*, far less cut corn in weather like that. I forget which member of an upper form later informed me loftily that they were Javanese women harvesting rice, but it still seemed to me to be unsound agricultural policy. In one corner of the room there was a round iron object which I jaloused to be a new-fangled stove because of the pipe which led up from it to the ceiling. Beside it was a blackboard on a four-legged easel – at least it had been black once but pale patches were beginning to appear on it like elbows through a jacket, and Miss Dalbeith seemed to spend most of her time scratching words on it for

65

George to repeat over and over again. Her own desk and high chair stood below a window which never closed winter or summer, and on our side of the room there were ten long desks each of them meant for five pupils; but seven of them had been vacant for many years.

There was a great tedium in not knowing English, so I spent some time scratching surrealistic pictures on my slate till the thing was full. I was wondering what to do about it when the girl beside me leant over confidentially and indicated that I should spit on my sleeve and rub. I did, and, lo and behold, the slate was like new. That was the second useful thing I learnt in school that morning, but I was to pay for it a few weeks later when Miss Dalbeith caught me at it and decided to teach me the word 'hygiene' with a cuff on the ear for every time I got it wrong. She was fanatical for hygiene, and in all the time I knew her, I never saw her use a handkerchief. Instead she ripped a piece from an old copy of *The Glasgow Herald* kept specially for that purpose . . . which she trumpeted into and then ceremonially burnt in the round black stove.

I was in the midst of rubbing out my umpteenth work of art when I became aware that a peculiar silence had fallen on the room, and when I looked around I found that George's English appeared to have deserted him. As the teacher's exhortations became shriller, George's face became redder. But it was total stalemate. And it ended only when an unmistakable word of command brought George shuffling to the front holding out his hand as if in reluctant greeting. For the first time in my life I saw two feet of leather strap being wielded by an enthusiastic and muscular woman. And I thanked God quietly that I had no English to forget.

The way that my first school-teacher could ply that belt would probably have earned her stardom in some deviant areas of today's sophisticated society. For all I know, Miss Dalbeith may have been a lonely disciple of the Comte de Sade, banished to a Hebridean outpost where the only deviations known were from the Ten Commandments which appear to have been carved in the days when men were men and women were women. Certainly there was an ecstatic gleam in her eye on that first morning of school as she leathered George for not knowing whatever it was he was supposed to know. For my own part, I watched the proceedings with a sinking heart, realizing that this was one of the things my mother had so often prophesied would happen to me when school began.

Whether or not it was sheer terror that brought the crisis on, I will never know. But, for the past few minutes I had been becoming aware of an increasing discomfort for which there didn't appear to be any solution in that particular green and yellow room. The uneasiness and the pressure increased with the knowledge that my neighbour was a girl whom I could not possibly consult, and if I couldn't ask Peggy in Gaelic how much less could I possibly ask Miss Dalbeith in the only language which she knew but which I didn't. By the time she noticed, the pool of my embarrassment was rivuletting its way towards her desk, and there was nothing she could do about it except splutter something that I couldn't understand . . . take me by the ear . . . and set me on the road for home. As I was going out through the gate, so much earlier than I had expected, I could hear her quelling the giggling which had been building up in my wake.

To this day I don't know why Miss Dalbeith let slip her first opportunity to use the leather 'Lochgelly' on me for what she must have considered a deplorable lack of self-control, but, fortunately for the tattered remains of my peace of mind the possibility of it didn't occur to me. I was too concerned with what my mother would have to say about the new Harris Tweed trousers that she had so painstakingly stitched for me and had put on me for school that morning for the first time – dry. All in all life seemed pretty bleak as I slunk past the workmen who were making our new road, and my face was hot from their banter about 'the boy who was expelled from school after only two

67

hours of education'. Looking up, I suddenly knew that all would be well; coming down the track into the village was my Grandfather whom I hadn't seen in months, leading my mother's belated dowry on a rope, in the shape of a black short-horn cow. The days of the crowdie and cream were about to start . . . as were the days of the bitter-sweet.

This was 'Big Grandfather' – all six-foot-two of him – who was married to my mother's dumpling little mother. (On the other side of the pedigree, the situation was totally reversed – 'Big Grannie' being married to 'Wee Grandfather' – which probably explains why I've come through life labelled 'Height – medium', a description for which one is only grateful if one is being sought for a crime . . . But be that as it may, it was a good thing for a boy to grow up with two intact generations ahead of him, and to be the first grandson was just fine!) Instead of turning into the new house, I ran straight up the hill to Grandfather and explained my indignity to him – and my predicament. I can't remember what he said but he made it all seem very unimportant as he swung me on to Daisy's broad black back – steaming hot and sweaty from her long walk. 'Look at the boy's new trousers – soaking from that cow's back,' said my mother as I was lifted off at the door. And the old man winked at me, and neither of us had to tell a lie.

Daisy was, as I said, my mother's belated dowry, and I stress the *belated* lest anyone wonder why my mother should be receiving a wedding present on the day that her first son was starting school. In those days, it was the custom for the bride's parents to give their daughter a start in married life by giving her a cow in calf on her wedding day. But that hadn't been possible in my mother's case because, when he came back from the war in 1918 my father had no land.

That was the first visit of 'Big Grandfather's' that I can remember, and I probably remember it because of the way he took things in hand. My mother was the youngest of his daughters, and maybe he resented the fact that she was the first to leave the nest in the same way as Laban was loathe to lose Rachel. Maybe I was just witnessing the age-old jockeying for position between the wife's father and a new son-in-law. Or, on the other hand, it may have been that he quite genuinely believed that my parents were incapable of bringing up children although he lived to see them bring up two more than he had done. Whatever it was, in the early days, he gave every appearance of being in charge, and that suited me very well; the threat of 'just you wait till your grandfather goes away' hung over me lightly, but in the event of any trouble I stuck closely by his side.

In the early autumn days, Daisy would spend her nights outside, tethered to keep her away from our first crop of corn, and my Grandfather felt it his duty to stay on to supervise the building of a byre for her against the coming of winter. Perhaps my father could have built it for himself, but I have a feeling that the old man suspected that he would never get round to it in time, because there runs in the paternal stream of my ancestry an inclination to . . . not necessarily to procrastinate, but to get side-tracked into lotus lanes. My father's obsession was with reading, and it was one that wasn't easily satisfied in a community far removed from libraries, and into which the newspapers were only beginning to percolate by post. The fact that they were a week old didn't matter because in those pre-wireless days topical stories were none the less welcome because they were mature.

Sometimes my father, slightly self-consciously, would lose himself in an aged copy of *Woman's Weekly* or *The People's Friend* which the minister's widow would hand on to my mother for their knitting patterns. But his salvation was Gibbon's *Decline and Fall of the Roman Empire*, which he made a point of reading once a year from the day he bought it, and his tattered copy of Macaulay's *Lays of Ancient Rome* which he read aloud to me till I knew 'How Horatius Kept the Bridge' off by heart before Miss Dalbeith had got me as far as 'The Cat Sat On The Mat', which is precisely what my new cat didn't – because my Great Aunt Rachel had sat on it. But that's another story.

Big Grandfather didn't approve of his son-in-law's literary bent, particularly during the hours of daylight each one of which he thought, like Kipling, should be used to the last second. My father was willing enough to labour and hold posts straight while the old man (who must have been all of fifty-five) architected and ordered and designed. And if anybody went against Grandfather's way of thinking he took an attack of sore feet and hirpled into the house for tea and sympathy till it was agreed that, maybe, his way was correct after all. Whereupon he made spectacular recoveries and hustled on with the job in hand.

It was in the evenings that my father came into his own. Being an inveterate 'reader-out-aloud' he revelled in bringing Grandfather up to date with the news from the least ancient of the newspapers to his hand. And whatever the news was – if it was serious – it always got a mention in Grandfather's prayers when, by virtue of his seniority, he took 'the books' as we called prayers at the end of the day. Not that the old man couldn't read for himself – otherwise he couldn't have coped with the mandatory psalm and chapter from the Bible, but, in the early years that I remember him, he confined his reading to *Cooper's Little Red Book of Sheep Management* and the Bible; he knew both pretty well by heart, which showed in his remarkable ability to open the Bible at a chapter appropriate to the news items which my father had imparted to him. A hurricane in the Pacific would automatically guide him to the Lord quelling the tempest on the Sea of Galilee, while at the news of an earthquake in Peru he would light upon the collapse of the walls of Jericho.

Unlike my father, who must have tested God's hearing to the uttermost, my Grandfather prayed sonorously and aloud, but as my education cumbersomely advanced I began to query the efficacy of praying for the safety of mariners in the aforesaid Pacific hurricane when, by the

70

time the newspapers reached us, their fate must have been decided one way or another anyway. But, on that particular visit, he seemed much concerned for the safety of men who, by their skills, were preparing to face the dangers of the skies. He prayed with such vehemence that I began to wonder on my aching knees if another flood was pending despite the rather ambiguous promise God had given when He put the rainbow in the sky.

It was only recently that curiosity made me try to find out what had so concerned the old man, and I discovered that, while he and my father were building that byre in Harris, away down in England men were putting the finishing touches to the R 101. I wonder if, away up there in the islands, the old man had some prescience of disaster. If he had it wouldn't be for the first or last time.

Chapter Eight

The only thing that marred that first visit of Grandfather's to our new house was the crisis which blew up in school. George had not taken his leathering meekly, and the very next day – my second day in the establishment – he had taken advantage of one of Miss Dalbeith's 'excuse me' absences from the classroom to dash to her desk and with unerring aim had flung her 'Lochgelly' high up through an open hatch in the ceiling and into the cobwebby darkness of the loft. It didn't take her long to discover her loss, and the interrogations which followed were of the type which anticipated by two decades the techniques developed to a finer art in the Third Reich.

By that second day in school I had learnt only two bits of English. One was that 'sit' meant 'sit'. And the other was that on the onset of the faintest feeling of discomfort in my nether regions I had to put up my hand and snap my fingers till I attracted Miss Dalbeith's attention and then say, parrot-wise, 'Please Miss, I want out'. It wasn't much to be going on with, particularly in the situation now developing which was obviously, in due course, going to embroil *me*. I have never been in an identity parade but I suspect that my feelings were like those of an innocent towards the tail end of the line who suspects that an accusatory finger may be pointed at him and that he may be totally unable to prove his innocence.

Miss Dalbeith started with the oldest boy in the school – a fellow who was a mere half-head shorter than herself and built like an ox. He was at a stage of manhood when the mothers in the neighbouring villages locked up their daughters when he did one of his occasional forays on the decrepit bicycle he had built himself out of bits and pieces; but his manhood was patently at a droop as he faced up to Miss Dalbeith's staccato. After an age she dismissed him and ordered him to the far end of the room, to stand on one leg with his back to the wall. The parade to the desk continued and, one after the other, in descending order of age the suspects were harangued and obviously threatened with dire consequences and then duly sent to join the lengthening queue of delinquents standing for all the world like bedraggled storks against the wall. Having seen George dispose of the strap through the opening of the loft I had a fair idea what the to-do was about, and I was impressed with the air of injured innocence with which he faced up to his ordeal before joining the queue at the wall. I myself wasn't unduly perturbed because I felt fairly immune behind my ignorance of English – there was obviously little that I could contribute to the drama on a vocabulary of 'sit' and 'Please Miss I want out'. But I reckoned without the resourcefulness of Miss Dalbeith.

Peggy was my immediate predecessor in the dock, but instead of being sent to the wall at the end of her interrogation she was kept back beside Miss Dalbeith who beckoned to me. As I went out I could sense the tension in the room mounting, and I could feel twelve pairs of eyes boring into my back; there was no doubt that I was being regarded as the weak link at the tail end of the chain of resistance. Miss Dalbeith turned to Peggy and delivered a long sentence.

Peggy turned to me and said in Gaelic, 'She wants to know if you saw anyone stealing her strap and if you don't say "no" the boys will kill you after school. Shake your head.' So I shook my head.

Miss Dalbeith was obviously losing heart and her next question was softer and shorter and, once again, Peggy interpreted as follows: 'You're doing very well. She wants to know if you know it's a sin to tell lies. Nod your head.'

So I nodded my head.

It must have been the blush that rose to my cheek at Peggy's compliment that convinced the teacher of my innocence because she indicated that I should return to my desk in solitude while Peggy took up her one-legged stance at the wall. I felt very warm towards Peggy for the way in which she had softened my ordeal for me. She was, even then, a strikingly beautiful girl with blue eyes and the jet black hair of the Iberian/Celtic race – her appearance, if anything, enhanced by a set of gleaming white, but protruding teeth. A few years later I was to kiss her on a cold and frosty Hebridean beach, and it was an experience which came back to me much later on in manhood when I bit into my first Baked Alaska.

Anyway, that was the second day of school, and also the end of the week because, then, new terms always began on a Thursday. For me, and a couple of other monoglots, a pleasant week-end stretched ahead. Not so for the rest. Having failed to illicit any information about the missing tawse Miss Dalbeith issued one of her standard punishments to the rest of the school. They were to come back on Monday morning with the whole of Psalm 119 learnt off by heart, and with the solemn assurance that each slip of memory would incur one stroke of the belt – the new belt which Miss Delbeith assured us she would have procured by then. For those who are not well up in the Scottish metrical psalms I should, perhaps, explain that 119 is the longest of King David's many compositions and must have been composed during a year when the lambing was poor or affairs of state were not pressing. It is over five hundred lines long, and somewhat lacking in continuity, and the devilishness of the punishment was that it would involve the entire literate section of the community since even the most advanced pupils were not totally fluent in English and would have to seek parental or friendly advice on words like 'statutes' and 'testimonies' and 'precepts'.

Miss Dalbeith, in all fairness, added one codicil – that, in the event of anybody accruing more than six penalties, the balance would be spread out over an appropriate number of days. She was thorough. Very thorough. But she made one mistake. She informed us triumphantly that she personally would contact Calum the Post and arrange for him to bring her a new strap on the Saturday morning and that it would be ready and waiting and locked in her desk come Monday morning.

Calum the Post was one of us, and Miss Dalbeith was a foreigner: she came from somewhere on the wrong side of the Minch and didn't speak Gaelic. Calum knew all the regulations of the Post Office off by heart and by Saturday evening the village knew that the postman had informed Miss Dalbeith that, much as he would like to oblige her, the rules forbade him delivering anything which did not come through the normal Post Office channels bearing a normal Post Office stamp. And so we breathed again, knowing that, between the uncertainty of the mail in those early days and the self-controlled uncertainty of Calum's memory there was little chance of Miss Dalbeith being armed for at least a week. And so it turned out.

Calum the Post, as I've just said, knew all the Post Office rules by heart. He also, doubtless, knew the Ten Commandments, and if he could adjust the laws of Moses then there would seem to be little reason why he couldn't put occasional variants into the laws of the Postmaster General.

Long before the threats of energy crises prompted some enlightened government to dream up the idea of combining the delivery of mail with the transport of passengers in thinly populated rural areas, we had a Mail Bus of our own. But nobody ever heard about it because Calum the Post would have lost his job, and that would have been a bit pointless because the weight of public opinion would have made his successor carry on where he left off anyway. The only difference between now and then was that our Mail Bus was a large red van with a large gold coat of arms painted on its side and the words Royal Mail in black. It was provided by the Government to travel northwards up the west coast of Harris every Tuesday, Thursday and Saturday delivering letters and parcels to the straggle of new croft houses. And on Mondays, Wednesdays and Fridays it travelled south picking up what was optimistically known as Outgoing Mail. For the latter purposes the Post Office also provided red pillar boxes – with GVR embossed on them so heavily that it suggested Royal immortality – into which the villagers were meant to pop their letters for Calum the Post to collect at the precisely stipulated hours on his southward journey. In those halcyon, pre-vandalism days the idea had obviously been proved to work in well organized places like Inverness and Islington, but it was different in Scaristavore.

For several reasons. First of all, those of the villagers who could write didn't have any compelling reason for doing so, except on the rare occasions when they wanted to order goods from the Mail Order Warehouses of the mainland, and when they did write they never had any stamps and it was easier to waylay Calum at the croft gate and hand him a penny ha'penny and the letter. Another reason for writing might have been to ask after the health of one's relatives, but that was a cumbersome way of going about things when one could get news from Calum not only of one's own but of other people's relatives as well. And then, of course, it became quickly obvious to everybody that it was a waste of government money to have a large red van trundling up and down the road with a few letters, a couple of parcels and a lot of empty space when a sack of seed potatoes needed to be transported from one croft to another, or a half-hundredweight of oatmeal had to be brought from a store nine or ten miles away . . . or even when an illicit salmon had to be taken from the vicinity of the landlord's river to a more deserving destination. At times of funeral or festivity the van could take up to a dozen passengers at a time, and while it was illegal for Calum to carry them it would have been even more illegal to charge them . . . and highly impractical for him to consider sticking them with penny ha'penny stamps.

Calum the Post was an immense personality. By law, he was supposed to stop his van at each croft gate if he had mail to deliver – lock the van and walk up to the house with his packages. But such servitude would have been undignified for someone who had probably been a corporal when our men were privates or matelots. And so, instead, he blasted his klaxon horn till somebody went down to the van to collect a letter or hear a bit of news. Only at two houses did he observe the law. At the Manse, and, of course, at the Schoolhouse where Miss Dalbeith would have reported him if he hadn't personally delivered the *Glasgow Herald*s into which she blew her nose.

Calum had a great heart and a good memory, and rarely did he pass a house without something to deliver – if not a letter, an ounce of tobacco or half a pound of baking soda or cream of tartar where these had been omitted from the weekly parcel of groceries. And the villagers, in their turn, dug him out of ditches when he went off the road, and straightened his mud-guards when he went too near a dyke, and they all took a personal pride in the certificate he received for careful driving after he had been twenty-five years on the road. Round about the middle of December Calum would begin to remind people gently that Hogmanay was drawing near, with a forecast that there was going to be 'a shortage' but that he himself might be in a position to help a friend should a bottle or two be required 'at the old price'. He was too honest to suggest that the price was going up, but there was something galvanizing about the phrase 'the old price', even in those days, and within a week his order list would be complete. And then, round about Christmas, he would begin to fall slightly further and further behind with his delivery schedule.

Not because he was bowed down with today's kind of excessive Christmas mail, but because he seemed to take it into his head that he should observe Post Office regulations for a trial period – taking selected houses in turn. He ceased to blow his horn and, instead, would in regulation fashion get out of his van and lock it and walk up to the door carrying under his arm a parcel which had never seen a sorting office. It embarrassed him to have to accept the price of the order, meticulously ticked off in his little red notebook (which, like the van, had GVR on the cover), and it really pained him to have to accept a glass in reward. But he always succumbed graciously, and he always removed the Crown's hat before bending the Crown's law. And so, he worked his way along the route, careful never to supply more than two or three houses on the one day lest his glasses of reward made him falter in the service of King George.

Ah well! He's been up there many years now, has Calum, and I often think that he must smile to himself and give his red-piped blue halo a tilt backwards when he sees his successors in the Mail Bus service punching tickets and accepting money for the things he did for our village for free.

Chapter Nine

I have never been able to discover the formula by which the Board of Agriculture, in far away Edinburgh, selected the eight successful candidates for the new crofts. For sure they were all ex-servicemen, but that was the only thing they had in common, and there must have been scores of disappointed applicants with that particular qualification. In the cities now, there is a tendency to allocate council houses on a 'points' system which would seem to favour couples of proven fertility and infinite patience and, occasionally, discreetly corrupt cousins in high places. But there doesn't seem to have been any obvious code of conduct or misconduct applied to the plantation of our village, and, in two or three cases, crofts had been allocated to bachelors who, for all that anybody knew, might have turned out to have neither the will nor the ability to guarantee the succession.

In the event the Board's judgement turned out to be sound, and, in due course, the bachelors succumbed in turn either to the urgings of their loins or the persuasions of inconvenience. But the man who started off the procession to the altar was not a crofter at all, but a man called James who lived with ageing parents in the old village and who had been known for some time to be courting my father's cousin Mary. Cousinage is a relationship which is carried to extremes in the Hebrides, and Mary was not the daughter of any of my father's uncles or aunts but she was of the same stock as Great Aunt Rachel and that was good enough. James was in the same sort of relationship to Gillespie and it was from the latter that I heard first that there was going to be a pre-wedding party to which everybody in the neighbourhood appeared to be invited except himself and myself, and, of course, my brother and his sister who were too young anyway. Needless to say we both vigorously challenged the manifest unfairness of the whole thing but we were told very firmly that the occasion was 'not suitable' and that was that.

The party began to assume extremely puzzling dimensions in our imaginations when it transpired that it was obviously going to be 'not suitable' for James either, and that he was going to be the 'looker after' (the word 'baby-sitter' had not been invented, far less translated) of the four of us, and that, to facilitate matters, Gillespie and his sister were to spend the night in our house. It was unheard of! People just didn't spend nights in other people's houses unless they were grandfathers or such! As the days wore on and the subject of the party took up more and more of playtime discussion in school, it turned out that Gillespie's information had not been wholly accurate and that, in fact, only the three or four oldest pupils were being invited and then only for the earlier part of the proceedings. That mollified us a little. But not wholly. Our other uninvited contemporaries lived much further away and the party wasn't on their doorsteps. Nor were James and Mary related to them.

At last the evening arrived, and, with it, feverish activity. Daisy was milked early. Gillespie and his sister were delivered to our house and fed. My father got into his navy-blue serge Sunday suit, and mother into a frock which I didn't even know existed. At some stage or other she laid out the two younger ones side by side, cross-wise, in the double bed normally occupied by my brother and myself and, alternately threatening and wheedling, she obtained promises from Gillespie and me that we would obediently climb in beside them as soon as James so decreed. If we were good, she promised, James would let

80

us stay up a little later than usual. Little did she know it but that was the last thing we wanted.

'O Lord,' said my father, 'here comes James taking the width of the road!'

It was an expression I hadn't heard before, but a quick glance through the window soon clarified it. James was a hero of mine for many reasons, but principally because he frequently took me for rides 'cross-bar' on his bicycle of which he was immensely proud and on which he was an expert. Tonight, though, his flickering carbide lamp was pursuing a decidedly erratic course along a road which was so moonlit that a lamp was totally unnecessary in the first place. However, by the time he came through the door he was impeccably sober as only a consciously inebriated man can be.

'You'll be all right, James?' said my father in a half questioning tone obviously meant to reassure himself if nobody else.

'Certainly,' said James.

'You needn't be bothering with the fire,' said my father, carefully closing the doors of the Modern Mistress.

'Not to worry,' said James producing his cigarettes, 'I've got matches.'

My father paled slightly, but my mother took his arm and oxtered him out through the door before he could begin to have third thoughts.

'You'll find milk and sugar and everything in the cupboard, James,' she threw over her shoulder as she closed the door behind her.

'Nothing like milk. Very good for one,' muttered James to nobody in particular as he sat down carefully on the red kist at the end of the table and began to arrange a half bottle of whisky, two packets of Capstan Full Strength and a box of Swan Vestas on the new oilcloth. 'James will look after the boys, won't he, boys?' and as if to underline his best intentions he produced two large bars of Toffee Cow as we called the succulent bars of MacCowan's Highland Toffee which were the vogue at the time and which must

81

surely have been the inspiration for the 'lock-tite' glues against which television adverts were to warn future generations.

'All right then, boys, time for bed!' said James as soon as he heard the gate squeak shut behind my parents.

'My mother said that we could stay up late if we were good and we haven't done anything.'

We wanted to go to bed early, but not yet.

'What your mother said was that you needn't go to sleep early but that doesn't mean to say that you don't have to go to bed.'

Sheer semantics! The phrase my mother had used could, indeed, be twisted to mean what he said, but the plan we had worked out was designed to allow us to keep James company for as long as possible rather than that we retire and risk falling asleep. And we wanted James to be so fed up with our company that he would be glad to see the last of us. Under no circumstances did we want him coming into the bedroom to check on us once we had gone through.

'My mother doesn't let me eat toffee in bed in case I choke.'

Gillespie's ingenuity took my breath away. I knew that toffee was as much of a rarity in his home as it was in my own, and that the chances of there being any left over at bedtime were slim indeed.

'Very well then!' He was getting snappy, which was just fine. 'Get on with your toffees; I'm going out to the end of the house.'

We could tell by the sound of his feet on the one little gravel patch at the door of the porch that he hadn't gone to the end of the house so we got on our knees on the bench and lifted our separate corners of the blind. James was on his way to the roadside gate and, for a moment, we thought that he was going to get on his bicycle and go away.

'No,' said Gillespie. 'His bottle of whisky is still on the table.'

James fumbled around his bicycle for a few moments and then lifted a parcel, which had obviously been strapped to his carrier; this he proceeded to lay on the dyke and unwrap. There was enough moonlight for us to see him lift to his mouth a glinting bottle of the type known as a screw-top. We wondered quietly to each other why he hadn't brought it into the house along with his half-bottle of whisky. But whatever his reasons, he was in no hurry to return to us and he continued to take long leisurely pulls till, presumably, the bottle was empty, when he swung it round his head a couple of times and flung it far away on to the machair. He glanced in the direction of the house but obviously didn't notice anything untoward with the blind which we didn't have time to replace. Thus satisfied, he took a second screw-top out of the parcel and rammed it into his breast pocket. He then scrumpled up the paper and jammed it into a niche in the dyke.

When he came back in we were sitting just as he had left us, chewing away at our Toffee Cow. He sat down at the end of the table keeping his arm carefully crooked over the bulge in his jacket.

'Is that a screw-top you've got in your pocket, James?'

He looked taken aback for a moment and then decided to laugh it off.

'Dash me, yes. I'd forgotten about it.' He took it out and put it on the table beside the whisky. 'Aye. Yes. Well you see – I didn't want them to think I might be drinking when I was looking after the two of you. Parents are very old-fashioned you know. I know fine that you two are perfectly able to look after yourselves, and I thought I would just be having a wee drink if I got lonely after you went to bed. That's reasonable enough isn't it?'

Gillespie and I had long since learnt to distrust adults when they were trying to sound reasonable so we said nothing. James lit a cigarette, and there was silence for a while.

'Why aren't you at the party?'

'Och it's just an old custom. The man who's going to get married is never at the *reiteach*.'

'What's a *reiteach*?'

'It's a party that's held a few nights before the wedding just to make sure that everything's all right and people bring presents and things like that. It's an old custom.'

'Is Mary going to have a baby?'

That startled him.

'Who did you hear saying that?'

'Is she going to have a baby?'

'Of course she's not going to have a baby! People don't have babies before they marry.'

'Marsail MacInnes isn't married or anything and she's got twins!'

'That's different! And will you stop pestering me! Where does your mother keep the glasses?'

'She hasn't got glasses.'

'Where does she keep the bloody cups then?'

He strode over to the big cupboard and began to fiddle with the key. As soon as his back was turned I closed the damper on the *Modern Mistress* so that peat smoke began to wisp into the room. James finally got the cupboard open and found a row of tumblers staring him in the face.

'I thought you said—' He broke off as he turned round and saw the smoke by now billowing from the range. 'What the devil have you done now?'

'I'll tell my mother you were swearing and drinking whisky and beer.'

'You'll tell your mother bugger all of the sort or I'll screw your neck for you and I'll never give you a ride on my cross-bar again. Now get into that bed and if I hear one word out of either of you I'll come through and bang your heads together till you're unconscious. Get going!'

He slammed the tumbler on the table and turned his attention to the stove.

'Leave the door open so that we have light to see to take off our clothes.'

'I'll leave the door open till I get this damn stove fixed and then I'm closing it for the night whether you have your clothes off or not!'

We could hear him twiddling the damper as we climbed into bed fully clothed and pulled the bed-cover up to our chins. In a few moments he came through and though we could only see his silhouette against the oil lamp in the living room we could tell by his voice that he was slightly surprised and considerably mollified to find us in bed.

'Good night, fellows', he said. 'You're not such a bad couple after all. I'll tell them how good you were.'

He closed the door. We waited till we heard the clink of a glass and, a moment later, the scrape of a match. We then slipped out of bed, swung open the bedroom window and set off for the party.

The first couple of hundred yards were exciting and then, as we got further and further into the moonlit emptiness I began to feel an inner cold creeping up on me that had nothing to do with the chill of the night. Now and again a puff of cloud would drift across the moon and I could feel myself flinching. I was just on the point of suggesting to Gillespie that it might be wise to forget the whole ploy when he turned to me.

'Are you – are you scared?' he whispered.

'Of course not,' I hissed back. 'Are you?'

'Of course not.'

That clinched it. The last moment for return had been squandered by each of us and now there was nothing for it but to press on.

'Let's run,' Gillespie gasped as we suddenly found ourselves in the shadow of the churchyard wall, and we set off as if every demon therein was on our tails. It felt like hours before we broke out of the shadows with our lungs bursting, and we could only stand and gasp when we finally gained the steely blue moonlight beyond. As we stood and fought for breath neither of us dared look back, and then, one of us spotted the light from Mary's home in the distance and the terror began to ebb away. We set off

85

at a jog trot and didn't pause again till we were a few yards from the door. Even at a distance the noise was deafening. It was a noise we had never heard before: the whole village joined together in the chorus of a raucous Gaelic song. We crept up into the shelter of the wall beside the door.

'How are we going to get in?' I asked Gillespie.

It was a question that had never occurred to either of us, but before we had time to debate it the door swung open and a young man and woman we didn't know slipped out hand in hand and tiptoed off in the direction of the barn on some private errand of their own, leaving the door of the house wide open behind them.

It was a big old-fashioned cottage which had once belonged to a gamekeeper or somebody of that standing, but Mary's old father now occupied it by virtue of being orra-man (ploughman, handyman, shepherd all rolled into one) to the landlord who had clung on to the home farm when the estate had been taken over and divided up. We were standing at the back door which led into a small scullery, past which we could see through another door into a turbulent mass of Sunday-best villagers swaying backwards and forwards between us and a huge white draped table loaded with food of a dozen kinds. We glanced at each other and I don't think we exchanged a word.

We dropped on our hands and knees and crept in through a jungle of legs whose owners, in retrospect, must have lost all feeling in them as we squeezed past. Somebody stood on my fingers and I nearly yelled with pain, but it passed in a flash as I pressed on. We hardly dared breathe as we squatted on the floor directly below the table, shielded, as we thought, by the drapes of the heavy linen cloth. I could just see Gillespie's face dimly in the half light below the table and, presumably, he could see about the same amount of me. We didn't dare speak but, from time to time, we gave each other triumphant little winks and smiles as the spirit of the evening began to percolate through to us. Apart from one cattle sale day and James, I had never seen anybody even remotely tiddly before, but I had heard disparaging conversations about drunkenness and had always understood it to be not a good thing. Here, however, it seemed to be epidemic and far from discouraged. The most used phrase of the evening seemed to be a slurred 'Come on, another wee one won't do you any harm', to which the recurrent response was 'Ach well . . .'

'Peter MacAulay, stand out here and give us a song, will you?'

Angels and ministers of Grace! Peter MacAulay was the prim, white moustachioed precentor, or leader of the praise in Church, and he was reckoned not much good at that. On one occasion, the minister, in deference to some visiting Englishman who had dropped in on a Gaelic service, had persuaded Peter to lead the congregation in the Old Hundredth Metrical Psalm which begins

> All people that on earth do dwell
> Sing to the Lord with cheerful voice . . .

When Peter protested that he didn't know a tune that would fit, he had been persuaded that Robert Burns's 'Banks and Braes of Bonnie Doon' would fit fine. Thus assured, Peter had embarked on the most hallowed of the psalms only to get carried away with himself to produce an excellent opening which went

> All people that on earth do dwell
> How can ye bloom sae fresh and fair . . .

before the minister could tactfully interrupt and take over the duty of precentor himself.

But here now was Peter (having silenced his wife's protestations) in full flight with a Gaelic wedding song which was, in today's terms, 'explicit' in the extreme, bringing half-hearted protests from the women and roars of approbation from the men. It went on for verse after

87

verse, and it was beginning to pall on me because its innuendo (if that isn't too delicate a word) was far above my head, although, as the years went on and the inevitable prurience of adolescence asserted itself, I was able to recall and relish swathes of it long after it had been forgotten by the rest of those present on that night.

Song followed song. Somebody played the bagpipe, and somebody played the trump as the Jew's Harp was called. Now and again Donald John Murray was prevailed on to lay down his drink and pick up his melodeon and the company erupted into dancing which involved frequent lurchings into the table. I was beginning to feel bored and sleepy when I felt the linen table cloth rustling at my ear, and I looked round to find a horny hand which I couldn't possibly identify waggling two slices of sponge cake in my face. I nudged Gillespie and we hesitantly took a slice each and munched – waiting with each bite for our presence to be announced and Nemesis to strike. But no. From then on, from time to time, the table cloth would rustle and the hand would appear – sometimes with a rock cake, sometimes with a leg of chicken, sometimes with a slab of currant cake and, now and again, with a mug of fizzy drink. Just a hand with a gold signet ring which seemed to be held in place on the pinkie by a large brown wart. At first it was a weird sensation to be establishing a relationship with a disembodied hand, but, fairly quickly, inhibition vanished giving way to a certain sense of security.

'Silence!'

I cringed. The voice was my father's. And all my rock cakes and chicken legs and fizzy drinks seemed to solidify cold in my stomach as I thought that he was going to sing. Because I knew that he couldn't.

But no. Instead he assumed to himself a strange and pompous voice which was untypically forceful and, truth to tell, rather pleasantly lubricated.

'My friends', he said, 'the time has now come!'

The time! The time for what? I looked at Gillespie and,

to my horror, found that he was slumped on the floor sound asleep. If the time had come to go home we were in serious trouble because our plan had been to be away and safely in bed before anybody knew that we'd been out of it. But it wasn't that. It became quickly clear that some new ploy was afoot, as my father, by dint of reason and persuasion and hectoring managed to divide the motley throng into two groups in such a way, happily, that I was left a clear, uninterrupted, worm's eye view of the far end of the room where Mary's old father, looking even more venerable than usual with his white goatee beard, neatly trimmed, stood erect and patrician looking, with his roly-poly wife clinging, apple-faced and twinkling, to his arm. I found it in my heart to feel sorry for them if they were going to be made fools of in anything resembling the way that the rest of the company seemed bent on making fools of themselves. But they seemed quite composed and, indeed, Mary's mother, judging by the beam on her twinkly-wrinkly face, was enjoying her glisk of the limelight.

My father, having got the company ordered to his satisfaction, launched into a measured, flowery, speech. On behalf of himself and everybody within and outwith the parish he thanked the old couple for their hospitality, and for 'the use of their roof', as he put it, for one of the best parties he had ever attended. Now, he wondered if they would extend their kindliness and good-will still further and receive a stranger who had arrived unexpectedly at the door.

Mary's father bowed graciously and said that his home had ever been open to the stranger and asked that this one should be brought forward. A man who was, indeed, a stranger to me stepped forward and bowed gravely to Mary's parents. My heart turned over when he held out his hand to the old man and I saw a glint of gold ring on his pinkie. I didn't need to look a second time to ascertain whether or not the ring was being held in place by a wart because gold signet rings just didn't sprout on the pinkies of our crofters. I was convinced that this was going to be the moment of betrayal and was trying to make up my mind whether to waken Gillespie or make a break for it on my own when the stranger began to speak. And if my father had been flowery, this fellow was worse. It turned out that he was a sailor home on leave and though he had been at parties in every corner of the globe this was, by far, the best he had ever enjoyed and he was sorry to be the one to introduce a note of solemnity into the proceedings.

'I am here', he went on, 'representing my good friend James, at whose shoulder I will be standing if and when the day comes that he gets married. James himself cannot be here tonight because he is practising the great art of looking after children, and it is to be hoped that he is learning well in case the day comes when he was to tuck in his own...' A great roar of laughter. The stranger appeared to glance at his shoes as he waited for the hilarity to subside but, in fact, he was looking me straight in the eye as I cringed under the table.

Resuming his speech he went on to explain that he had been sent, because of his great experience of boats and the sea, to buy a boat for James! It had to be a good boat – a boat that had not been ill-treated in any way; a boat that could stand a tall mast; a boat that would last well and would not be expensive to maintain... It was a long speech, made longer by the gales of laughter that greeted every apparently innocent sentence, and he described a boat that was out of this world.

'And finally', concluded the stranger in his smooth Gaelic, 'it must be known to you that my friend James is a man of great experience with boats (howls of laughter from the company) and a man who knows a good boat when he sees one and will not be taken in by paint and varnish! I am asking, therefore, if you can sell me a boat that is sound from prow to stern (more laughter), one that will stand up to whatever weather comes her way, and will not ever drag her anchor.' The stranger gravely acknowledged the applause and stepped aside.

90

Mary's father stroked his beard and held a serious whispered conversation with his wife. He then moved slowly forward and took my Great Aunt Rachel by the hand. She was creased with laughter and I noticed that she had put her teeth in for the party. 'Here', said the old man, 'is a boat which has weathered many storms, but she's good for a few years yet. As far as we know she's only ever had one mast (complete uproar) and only her present owner has ever hoisted her sails.' (Pealing laughter again.) 'This boat has been well cared for. She may look weather-beaten but her beam is sound!'

It was some time before the stranger could reply, but when he did it went something like this: 'A fine boat I have no doubt but not suitable for the shallow waters around these parts. Top heavy too unless my eyes deceive me. But, worst of all, old boats have characteristics of their own and they are not always obedient to a new hand on the rudder. No. If you can't do better than that I must look elsewhere.'

My Great Aunt Rachel squeezed herself back into her armchair with her bosom heaving and tears of laughter streaming down her face. I took advantage of the applause to shake Gillespie awake, and clapped my hand over his mouth before he could ask where he was. For the rest of the pantomime he crouched on his hands and knees looking mystified.

Mary's father proceeded to bring forward, one after the other, four or five women from the neighbourhood although, mercifully, not Gillespie's mother or my own. And one after the other the stranger turned them down – sometimes with ribald comment where the candidate was a buxom adolescent; with great graciousness where she was a modest matron. At last he seemed to lose patience and made as if to go, but before he could do so Mary's father took his daughter by the wrist and pulled her, protesting coyly, into the ring.

'Very well,' he said, 'this is my last offer to you. Here is a boat I have always meant to keep for myself. But if your

91

friend James will promise to look after her I might consider letting her go.'

The stranger beamed. He took Mary and spun her round and round, pretending to be running his hands over her but not touching her at all. 'My friend', he said at last, 'this is the very boat for James, and, if I mistake not, perfect for the kind of cargo he has in mind for her...' As the laughter began to well up again, my common sense told me that it was time to make our get-away; I tugged a bemused Gillespie by the sleeve and we began to thread our way on hands and knees back through the legs.

Outside, the gibbous moon had worked its way round so that the kirkyard wall no longer cast a shadow, and we sped past it in silence. Gillespie, having missed the first Act, could have had no clue as to plot or denouement: I myself had only a vague feeling that, by a combination of sense and good luck, his friend had done well by James. What I was not to realize till much later was that I had been privileged to witness an old Highland wedding custom that I was never to see again.

We found the bedroom window ajar as we had left it, and after we had climbed out of our clothes, leaving them in a heap in the middle of the floor, we eased open the living-room door. The half bottle was lying empty on the table, the tumbler beside it with half an inch still left in it. The top of the Modern Mistress was littered with ash and cigarette ends. And on St Clement's bench lay James, snoring, satisfied that he had discharged his duties, and blissfully unaware of how close he had come to finding my Great Aunt Rachel standing waiting for him at the altar.

Chapter Ten

On the morning after the *reiteach* my father was not his usual easy-going self, and, from behind the heavy tweed bedspread which he had pulled up to his eyes he sustained an acrimonious interchange with my brother and Gillespie's sister who had been gallumphing through the house since dawn. Not unnaturally they were curious to know why James, fully dressed, was sound asleep in our living room. Was he sick? My father hoped so. Would James be all right in a wee while? My father hoped not.

At last my mother couldn't keep quiet any longer.

'For goodness' sake leave the children alone; they haven't done anything to you. Your own mother's sister warned you last night what you'd be like if you didn't take it easy, but . . .'

'Rachel thinks she's just got to put her hat on and her teeth in and she's God Almighty. In any case I'm not looking for an argument; I'm just telling those children to keep quiet while I get some sleep. Is that too much to ask?'

'They're hungry', I volunteered. And I should have known that any suggestion from me would be inflammatory.

'Go and feed them then seeing you're so smart!'

'The fire's out.'

'Light it then!' He jerked up in bed. 'O God, no! What am I saying? Don't go near the fire or I'll flay the backside off you. Just go back to sleep everybody till it's time to get up in a wee while.'

He stretched out his arm from below the bedcover as he lay back on the pillow and brought the little tin alarm clock up to his face. He looked, and looked again, and in what was virtually one movement rammed the clock back on the cabin trunk by the bedside, flung the bedclothes back, reached for his shirt forgetting he still had it on, and swung his legs to the floor, looking slightly surprised to find that they were still in his long johns.

'It's eleven o'bloody clock and the cow hasn't been milked. What'll the neighbours think? It's Saturday and the postman will be here any minute and we'll be namely from here to Luskentyre.'

'Well I can't get up till you get James roused,' my mother mumbled. 'In any case I doubt if the postman'll be round today; he was still at the *reiteach* when we left and showing no signs of leaving.'

'He'd better be round with my *Weekly Scotsman* even if he's got to get someone to drive him.'

'Pappy, why are you putting on your Sunday trousers if it's Saturday?'

He glared at me and began to reverse out of his navy-blues. 'Since you're so damned clever get out of that bed and get into your own trousers and let the hens out and bring in a pail of water.'

I slid out of bed and Gillespie, who hadn't uttered a word, slipped out after me and, covering his manhood with one hand, began to struggle into his trousers. We wasted no time getting into our things, and though the water pail clanged like a tocsin as I picked it up on my way through the living room, James didn't stir. Out of the corner of my eye I noticed that a burning cigarette had obviously fallen out of his sleeping fingers at some point; a pencil of grey ash lay in a scorch mark on the floor. I had a feeling that James was in for a very rude awakening indeed.

My father needn't have worried about the village. There wasn't a trace of movement anywhere, nor a wisp of smoke from any chimney. But over the caged clucking of our own hens and Daisy's groaning, one could hear the protests of imprisoned animals from north and south. The *reiteach* had obviously paralysed the community at large.

After we had released the hens from their end of the byre and thrown them several handfuls of corn from the sack in the corner, we made our way to the 'well rock'. The word 'well' was the name for any source of drinking water, and the well rock was a large flat rock jutting into the river; whether the water was high or low some of it was channelled through a V-shaped gouge in the rock forming a spout below which one could hold a pail for filling. Usually I could manage three-quarters of the galvanized pail, which was a fair weight even when it was empty, but with Gillespie to help me we were able to fill the pail to its brim and thus, with any luck, save ourselves a second trip for a while. We were walking gingerly out of step, which is the only way to carry a bucket of water without slopping it, when we met James on his way from the house to the river with a towel draped over his shoulders. Save on the coldest of winter days all our less private ablutions were performed in a pool below the level of the well rock and even if a skliff of ice had to be broken from the surface, that was preferable to the chore of carrying pails of water into the house, pouring into a basin, and slopping out again.

'You're up, James!' we chirruped. But it was a fact of which he was oblivious or else was unwilling to concede, because he strode past us without glancing our way.

Miracles had taken place in our short absence. The empty bottle and the glass had disappeared. The floor was spotless apart from the pale brown scorch-mark which was to resist several attacks with *mealtrach* and sand before it finally vanished. There was a bright fire crackling in the grate which was gleaming black again. Not for the last time I marvelled how a woman can in a flash create tidiness out of chaos. Mother was standing with the lid off the kettle waiting for us to arrive, and father was collecting the milking jug and pail in readiness for the job he hated

95

most in life. He was still unshaven but his old imperturbability had returned.

'Be sure you strip her properly!' my mother said as she lifted the pail from us. A cow will very quickly go dry if her udder isn't completely emptied at each milking.

'Do I ever do otherwise?'

'When did you milk her last?'

But the tone of each was bantering, and it was reassuringly clear that life was getting back to normal. Or as normal as it could be with three extra people for breakfast.

'And to think that the wedding has still to come!' my father muttered as he went out.

The wedding still to come! I hadn't thought that one out.

'What does he mean, mother?'

'James's wedding, of course. That was only the *reiteach* last night . . . the preparation for the wedding. James and Mary are getting married next Friday.'

'Friday. When we're in school?'

'We're going to see about that. You and Gillespie sit at the table there with the wee ones, and I'll give you your brose when the kettle boils. I want you out of the way quickly so that I can get on with feeding your father and James.'

There were a whole lot of questions I wanted to ask, but we were interrupted by James who came back in from the burn looking slightly fresher but still tight-lipped. My mother smiled at him and took the towel.

'Sit down on the bench there James. I'll get you a cup of tea till the breakfast's ready. And don't worry. He didn't mean what he said. You won't make a lou – er – rotten husband for Mary, and he knows it fine. If only you hadn't let that cigarette burn the floor; he's terrified of fire since . . .' She glanced in my direction and stopped short.

'He sounded to me as if he meant every bloody word of it – especially the bit about five years in the army doing me good. It wasn't my fault that I was too young when the war ended. And I wasn't tupping women in the haystacks when he was in the trenches . . .'

'James! I won't have that language in front of the children. Sit down!'

'Tupping!' said my brother rapping his spoon on the table.

'See what I told you. He'll come out with that when Murdo Mor's in the house.' Murdo Mor was a kirk elder and very pernickety in his language as in his manner. James sat down and guiltily lit a cigarette, taking exaggerated care to put the spent match in the ash pan.

Father came back from the byre in due course, beaming with success and with the milk pail three quarters full. Daisy had obviously been so glad to get rid of her burden that she had refrained from lashing out at the pail at the last moment. He used to claim that she deliberately lulled him into a sense of security by chomping at her cud right up till the moment when the pail was full and then, when he was off his guard, she would either kick the pail over or stick her foot in it. He would never concede that the beast might possibly be getting bored with his amateur slowness.

Gillespie's father arrived to collect his children before breakfast was over, and he sat with a cup of tea reminiscing over the highlights of the *reiteach* and discussing the plans for the day of the wedding. It was his idea, I think, that the minister's widow should be approached to negotiate with Miss Dalbeith in the forlorn hope that the latter might be persuaded to give the school a day off on the day of the wedding – even if it meant having to invite her to the celebrations herself. She wouldn't last long, Gillespie's father thought, without a word of Gaelic in her head.

The idea worked. Miss Dalbeith agreed to close the school for the day – on condition that the pupils put in a full day's attendance on the Saturday. It was a mean and grudging concession in view of the fact that, weary or otherwise, parents would have to be early afoot – overhung or otherwise – to get their offspring to school for ten.

She declined her invitation with unwonted grace and, to everybody's surprise, announced that she would like to donate a present to the bride and groom. The surprise was compounded when the present was unveiled to reveal an original oil painting by herself – an impressionistic canvas portraying the hoary old legend of the Viking invasion of the Scarista beach in which the horned Norsemen, armed to the teeth with assegais and double-barrelled shotguns resembled, unmistakably, kenspeckle local worthies – the Black Shepherd, Murdo Mor and our gentle and much revered veteran of Mafeking and Mons.

Inevitably, Gillespie and I both independently let slip that we had been to the *reiteach*, and the reactions of our parents had been exactly the same. We were accused of telling lies and concocting fairy tales from snippets that we had overheard – and that was that. Even had we persisted there was a powerful witness against us in James, who would have sworn in a court of law that we were safe in our beds; so we didn't even have to be on our guard against slips of the tongue any more. In any case the week ahead was full to overflowing. Miss Dalbeith saw to it that the euphoria which was gripping the village did not infect the schoolroom, but in the evenings we were allowed to savour the excitement of the preparations which seemed to involve everybody, whether or not they were related to either Mary or James. I found my every moment taken up with chores even more tedious than usual and whenever I protested I was bribed with promises of being 'allowed to go to the wedding for a while'. It was long afterwards that it dawned on me that even the bribes were hollow: I would have had to be allowed to the party anyway because there wasn't a willing 'looker-after' available within the confines of six parishes!

One of the routines I had always minded least was feeding the hens. Our stock had risen to fourteen and two haughty and argumentative cockerels. The hens and one of the cockerels were White Leghorns, and the odd one out was the newcomer to the fold – a hefty Rhode Island

Red cock with a stride like a Guardsman and a crimson serrated comb which he wore like a royal hat. 'Joshua' was the name I had given him because, presumably, the name had caught my fancy during one of my Grandfather's Bible readings, and the rival Joshua was on the point of demolishing was just plain 'Doodle-doodle'. I was on excellent terms with the white hens, each of whom I knew personally by some name or other, and because I fed them so often they were all friendly with me; some of the older ones would even squat down when they saw me coming and allow me to tuck their heads under their wings and rock them till they went to sleep. They were part of my education too since it was with them that I had learnt to count up to fifteen – and then sixteen – long before Miss Dalbeith had got round to producing her multi-coloured abacus.

And so, on the Wednesday before the wedding, I only had to count twice to know that my brood had mysteriously shrunk to thirteen. Doodle-doodle was gone and so were two senior White Leghorns called Cailleach and Mairon. It was on the cards that Cailleach and Mairon had gone broody and taken themselves off to nest in some patch of bracken whence they might emerge in three weeks – each with a brood of a dozen fluffy chicks in tow. But it wasn't a very satisfactory explanation. It wasn't the right time of the year. And, most certainly, no such urge would overcome Doodle-doodle.

I ranged the croft banging my tin basin and chook-chooking at the top of my voice, but nothing happened and I was on the point of giving up when I heard an answering echo from the direction of the neighbouring croft. It was Gillespie, on the same mission of mercy as myself. It came out that he was three hens light too – or, to be more precise in his case two cockerels and a hen. We gave up after a while and decided that there was nothing for it but to report to our parents and face up to the blame which would, inevitably, be laid at our door. But, on the contrary! My mother showed no concern whatsoever. Nor would she volunteer any theory or explanation. Instead she switched me on to filling those interminable water pails, and after that I was to go and help my father at the byre. She herself was getting ready to go out for the evening, and would I please stop asking questions and do what I was told? And no, I couldn't go with her. And, for the last time, would I take myself off to help my father? And would I kindly take my brother with me from beneath her feet?

My father was behind the byre wrestling with a long bamboo fishing rod to the end of which he was tying a large white pillow case. He was in expansive form unlike my mother who had been unusually keyed up. He was, he explained, making a flag, and if we would just be patient we could help him fix it to the chimney stack when he was finished. And mother? Why, she was at the Hen Wedding and wouldn't be home till late. A Hen Wedding sounded a distinctly peculiar affair considering that the hens seemed, hitherto, to have conducted their marital cavortings without formalities of that order; but he was so engrossed with his flag that it was manifestly pointless to press him for further explanations. In the morning, he assured us, all would be revealed. In the meantime, the dark was fast coming on and would we please carry the ladder down to the end of the house. We did. And we watched, spellbound, as he climbed carefully to the top of the iron chimney stack and, using yard upon yard of coir rope left over from the corn-stacking, strapped the bamboo fishing rod to the chimney. When he was satisfied that it was secure he reversed down and removed the ladder. He stood with his head tilted back and a smile on his face. 'Look at that boys,' he said with pride, 'there won't be another flag like that in the village!' He was right. Just as he spoke a puff of wind blew into the mouth of the cotton pillow case which he had forgotten to stitch closed, and it swelled out into a big white sausage which might have been perhaps more aptly described as a 'wind sock' had there been aeroplanes around at the time. 'No,' he repeated, this time slightly ruefully I thought, 'there won't be one like it in the village right enough!' He reached for his pipe. 'I just hope', he said to himself more than to us, 'I just hope the wind doesn't get up or the chimney will be away!'

But the wind didn't get up, and when I looked out in the morning not only was our flag flying bravely, if slightly obesely, but there were flags flying above or beside every house in the village. Most of them were white pillow-slips like ours, but one or two were pink and, wonder of wonders, above the school there flew a Union Jack.

It was a long day. James and Mary and the best man and Mary's sister had set off for Stornoway in two hired cars. It was an extravagance which would not, normally, have been contemplated, but our own church was vacant and the village hadn't yet organized itself sufficiently to set in motion the complicated machinery for finding and inviting a new minister. It was a blessing in disguise, according to James's best man; by getting married in Stornoway – fifty miles away – they were spared the danger of the minister accepting an invitation to the festivities. 'Clergymen are fine for marriages, but bloody wet blankets at weddings', was the way he put it.

Fifty miles over our rutted roads represented a two-and-a-half-hour journey then, so – allowing for a marriage service with all the Presbyterian trimmings and admonitions and insurances against every possible eventuality of this life and the life to come, and a couple of hours for a meal in a hotel – the earliest that the villagers could expect the newly-weds back for the celebrations was six o'clock. And even at that there was the danger that daylight might be beginning to fade and that people might be deprived of the chance to cheer the bridal car back home. My brother and I were scrubbed and spruced by four o'clock and forbidden to put our noses outside the door till we had our parents' say so. They themselves had just begun to get dressed when one of 'the bloods' came racing to the gate on his bicycle and shouted that the car had been seen

101

coming into Tarbert where the couple had stopped for afternoon tea; this meant it would be arriving in the village in about an hour's time.

By five o'clock every family in the village stood in a finely arrayed knot at its own gate, and everybody, from the youngest toddler to the oldest Granny had a handkerchief or a pillow-case or a coloured scarf to wave – and Grannies and Grandfathers and sundry other relatives had descended on the village from all over the island. My own father's parents – Big Granny and Little Grandfather – had made one of their few trips south, but they had elected to stay with Great Aunt Rachel who had room to spare and, if truth be told, a large feather bed which suited Big Granny better than anything we had to offer. Not for all the tea in China would she have submitted herself to a made-up bed on St Clement's bench.

It was a beautiful evening with a late autumn brittleness in the air. It is a mainland presumption that autumn is a season of mellow browns and golds, with the earth giving back of the warmth it collected in summer. In the treeless islands it is different. For sure, here and there an intrusion of bracken may give a russet blush to a fallow sward, and a patch of ripened corn may reflect a glimpse of Keatsian sun; but the Hebridean autumn is the beginning of winter rather than the end of summer, and the mountains appear to be beginning to age and the sea to feel heavy. And there is a quality of silence as if the Heavens were drawing their breath for the storms. Set against such a background that childhood scene remains imprinted on the mind; and what could only have been a sprinkling of people, a little more colourfully attired than usual, against a vast landscape, has come to assume Lowrian proportions in a sprained memory. But the bagpipe was there, for certain, playing tirelessly and endlessly, and at its sweetest as it always is in the evening distance, whiling away the time as we waited for the car to crest the top of Back of Scarista Hill.

Then – horror! Three gates away I caught sight of

102

Kenneth Macleod squinting along the sights of a double barrelled shotgun!

I knew that Kenneth had been a suitor for Mary's hand, and that he had been alternately teased and consoled by people like my own mother when Mary had plumped for James. And here he was now, obviously out for revenge. I screamed at my father and tugged at his jacket, startling the living daylights out of him. He snatched me up thinking that some sudden hurt had come to me, and then burst out laughing when he heard my garbled fears. He explained that it was Kenneth's allocated duty, as the only owner of a shotgun, to fire a saluting volley over the car — and not at it — to welcome the married couple back; the Royal Navy, he added, did the same sort of thing on the occasion of the King's birthday but, so far, not one salvo had gone near the person of His Majesty. I felt slightly foolish, but relieved withal! In a few moments a shout went up as the car came over the hill, and people began to clap and cheer, and Kenneth began to shoot like a man in the front line.

In the normal course of events the wedding party – unlike the *reiteach* which was always in the bride's home – would have been in the couple's new house but, since James didn't have a croft of his own, he and Mary were going to live with his parents till either he got a croft or else decided to go back to sea. For the time being he was earning a living, like quite a few of the men in the district, working on the new road. It was in his parents' house that the Hen Wedding had been held the previous evening, and it was thither that the whole population of the village was wending its way now – not hurrying, so as to give the host and hostess a chance to spruce themselves up after their long day. A day which, according to all speculation was going to stretch well beyond the statutory twenty-four hours!

We were about the last to arrive and, at first, I thought we were never going to get in. The *reiteach* had been thronged, but this was mobbed with people from all the villages around. Individual invitations as such were unheard of then, and anybody who knew the bride or groom at all just arrived and was welcome; in fact, not to attend a wedding would have been insulting, and even people who were comparative strangers to the families made a point of making a token appearance with a gift. By the time we arrived the room was already steaming hot and throbbing with people and, for a while, it looked as if all I would ever see of the proceedings was yet another forest of legs. But somebody shouted 'Give the little ones a chance!' and we were lifted on to window sills, the sideboard and even broad shoulders.

From my particular vantage point I could see that several tables had been pushed together to form a large T-shape which occupied most of the room, and James and Mary – the one looking as flushed and self-conscious as the other – were already sitting in the middle of what would now be called the 'top table'. Glasses of all shapes and sizes were being handed around, and I was given a tumbler of red fizzy stuff which I had never seen before in my life. I scoffed it off, and the tumbler was promptly replenished. I was half way through that one when I noticed that nobody else was touching his, and I stopped with a guilty start. Murdo Mor, Kirk Elder and all as he was, was climbing on to a chair with a brimming glass of whisky in his hand. He was, as he said himself, 'going to make a speech to the bride and groom', whether people wanted to hear him or not. I didn't hear him, except that I was conscious of the fact that he kept repeating the phrase 'man and wife' and every time he said it people roared approval as if he had invented a sentence of stunning originality. My attention was focused elsewhere.

On the far side of the room I could see a long table, made up of two barn doors laid end to end on top of barrels, its whole length covered with the corpses of several dozen very naked and very cooked hens. It didn't require much imagination to jalouse that, on their backs with their legs raised heavenwards like the rest, there were two White Leghorns called Cailleach and Mairon and a cockerel called Doodle-doodle.

I felt sick.

'Where did all the hens come from?' I hissed to my father.

'Ssh!'

'Who cooked all the hens?' I insisted, not caring whether I was interrupting Murdo Mor or not.

'Your mother and the women, of course! What do you think the Hen Wedding was for last night? Will you shut up now!'

I shut up.

It was the first genuine act of betrayal that I was ever aware of. Conspiring in an act as opprobrious as hame-sucken, my own father or mother, or both, had stolen into the byre while I and the hens were all innocently asleep, and thrown the necks of three of my senior charges and plucked them and gralloched them and boiled them without as much as leaving a tell-tale feather! I felt my gorge rising, and would probably have sicked up my fizzy drink if there hadn't been, at that point, an explosion of applause as Murdo Mor finished speaking, and the room cascaded into a Gaelic song. When it was finished, the first thirty or so guests – the closest relatives – were called to the first sitting while the rest embarked on an orgy of whisky and song.

'Look!' said Gillespie who had sidled over beside me.

I followed his finger, and there, over in a corner balanced on what looked suspiciously like a pee-tub, was the school blackboard. But instead of being covered in the usual hieroglyphics it was loaded with trifles, and jellies and puddings for which I didn't have a name.

'They'll be all gone before they reach us,' said Gillespie.

But we needn't have worried. At the only village wedding which I ever attended, the ones who were best looked after were the very young and the very old.

Poor James and Mary. They sat at the head of that table through seven sittings that I saw, and they were still there, laughing and smiling when I was wakened at four o'clock in the morning to be carried, uncomplainingly home. It was a brilliant silver night, and the moon had fattened out since the *reiteach*. The flags were sleeping against their poles. I could hear the grumbling of the waves on the beach, which one never noticed during the day, and through it, receding in the distance I could hear the chorus of 'Horo my nut-brown maiden' being sung for the umpteenth time.

As I was pushed in between the blankets I had a passing thought that weddings were better things by far than Hogmanays, but, as I slid into peacefulness it never once crossed my mind that my feeling of well-being might be due in no small measure to two large helpings of White Leghorn hen.

Chapter Eleven

Birth, marriage, and death are the syntax of a community. Even in amorphous urban smothers their incidence draws together, sometimes for a rare occasion in a lifetime, people of forgotten bond – be it kinship or friendship or even childhood acquaintance – who have long since ceased to consort habitually, and, for a brief duration they become a community within the anonymity. But the effect of the wedding of James and Mary on us was an enduring, cementing one. Our eight crofter families had been drawn from different airts, and even if, perhaps, some of the men had met or known each other before, their wives had not; and since the village was strung out over three miles, and the women because of infant families were relatively housebound, they had remained distant neighbours and acquaintances without developing close friendships. But the *reiteach*, the Hen Wedding and the wedding itself had changed all that. The whole population had been thrown together in a prolonged proximity of celebration and co-operation, and the foundations of an identifiable community were laid down.

The festivities dragged on for a week, in much the same way as a Scottish Hogmanay tends to prolong itself into the New Year's maturity. And for the same reasons. It wasn't possible for the entire circle of friends and acquaintances to get together on the one night without bringing the economy of the island, such as it was, to a total standstill, to say nothing of letting cattle beasts and bedridden ancestors starve. There was nothing else on the scale of the wedding night itself, but James's parents were forced to keep open house for days, and a stocked larder and a supply of whisky against the arrival of friends and relations with gifts and thirsts.

The brand new couple went off to Glasgow for a week's honeymoon the day after their wedding, and as far as I could make out they just rose straight from the wedding table after the fourteenth or fifteenth sitting, changed into fresh clothes, and set off by yet another hired car to catch the *Lochmor* – our thrice-weekly ferry-boat to the mainland – at Rodel. That created a small stir. There were the inevitable derisory comments among the young men about James's lack of initiative, and how they would have gone about matters had they been in the bridegroom's place: they certainly wouldn't have spent the night sitting upright at the head of a table; it wouldn't have been the Minch they'd have been bouncing on next morning; and it wouldn't have been the *Lochmor* they'd have been aboard. From the fact that my mother kept 'tut-tutting' and shushing them up I guessed that some of their remarks were worth remembering for later understanding. The older folk thought a honeymoon an alien idea, to say nothing of an expensive one, and Great Aunt Rachel was heard to declare that the morning after her wedding she had been up to milk the minister's cow at seven o'clock as usual. Despite her undoubtedly strong personality and her forthright views, Great Aunt Rachel firmly believed that a woman's place was in the home, and one step behind her husband. She always addressed her husband as 'Man', in public at least, and he always addressed her as 'Woman', and if she had lived to see the dawn of the feminist movement the only thing she'd have thrown away would have been Germaine Greer.

We younger ones were brought firmly down to earth by having to go to school on Saturday – the morning after the wedding. Miss Dalbeith rattled her way through the attendance register as usual and every single name that was called responded with the usual 'Present, Miss', one of the first

English phrases hammered into every new recruit. One quick look round would have been enough to inform her whether anybody was missing or not, but that was her way of it. And in the event of somebody not being present, the person sitting next to him or her was expected to jump up and say 'Absent, Miss'. It may have been her way of ensuring that we learnt at least three English words. And we did. Because she went through the process first thing every morning and, again, first thing after the dinner break. God help the person who was declared 'Absent, Miss' at two o'clock; it was inconceivable that anybody should be overcome by ill health in the middle of the day.

We didn't do too much work that day – either because she regretted having to be on duty herself on a Saturday when she could have been indulging in her winter pastime of hillwalking, or, more likely, because her blackboard was still in James's father's house presumably not yet cleared of the remains of jellies and trifles. The morning passed wearily; the mid-morning break felt much longer than usual even though we all had tit-bits of information to exchange about the wedding, and the two oldest boys entertained us with some salacious bits of information anent what brides and grooms got up to once the festivities were over. It was that morning that I heard for the first time of a most mysterious piece of apparel called a 'French Leather', and, a year or two later it became, for reasons which I cannot for the life of me disentangle, confused with the word 'chamois'. In the mind. Not, fortunately, in any remote reality.

An uncomfortable shuffling of feet began to develop in the classroom as our stomachs, in the absence of anything resembling a clock or a watch, told us that it must be one o'clock and time for lunch. But nobody dared raise the question with Miss Dalbeith, and she, certainly, would not deign to inform us of her intentions. It felt like an eternity till she announced that it was now two o'clock, and that she would call the afternoon register and dismiss the school. She had made her point. She had observed the letter of the law and registered the two attendances that the School

Board expected of her, and should her books be examined by some officious minion of the Department of Education at some future date, they would show, in all truthfulness, that the 'scholars' of Scarista School had clocked in ten times that week! As far as we were concerned, the best of the weekend still lay ahead and she had forgotten to give us any homework. Even now I cannot credit her with the possibility that she might have refrained from doing so out of any spirit of goodwill.

There is nothing stranger than the things which stick in one's mind except the things which escape it. It is not, perhaps, surprising that I remember the wedding in vivid detail because it was, by any standards, a momentous landmark not only in my own small life but in the early life of the new village. Nor is it surprising that I remember Miss Dalbeith in such detail that if I were to meet her on Carter's Bar or in Wheeler's in Old Compton Street – which Heaven forfend – I would recognize her immediately and tremble. But curiously I cannot remember the first Christmas in the village, perhaps because it wasn't celebrated or accepted as a Presbyterian festival, nor, even more curiously, can I remember the first New Year, which was. I cannot remember ever going to Sunday School although I have, in front of me, an elaborate certificate signed by the minister's French widow crediting me not only with 'Regular attendance' but also with 'Good conduct', signed Adèle Kerr. I do, however, remember the day of Wee Barabel's funeral although I don't suppose there are many others who do, for the poor soul just slipped away in a ripeness of years that even she could not enumerate.

In addition to my Sunday School Certificate, I have also in my possession a silver medal and a copy of the *Concise Oxford Dictionary*, engraved and inscribed respectively, to testify that I had seven consecutive years of perfect attendance at school up to the time that I graduated, at the age of thirteen, to the delinquencies of what was then honourably called Junior Secondary School. I set out recently to discover why, if I was such a little masochist, I didn't have *eight* years

110

of perfect attendance which would have been the maximum possible in Primary School. It wasn't difficult to check because I have also, by means which matter not, the official Record of the 229 pupils who attended our particular brand of Public School from the day it opened on the 24th of July, 1893, till the day it closed forever, sixty years later, in 1953. And I discovered that all my defections took place in the reign on Miss Dalbeith, which proves that my masochism wasn't so devout after all. The last of these must have been at the end of winter or in very early spring because there was snow on the ground and I had acquired enough English to know what was going on.

I shouldn't have gone to school at all. I had wakened up with a miserable chesty cold, and my mother wanted me to stay in bed with a wadding of red flannelette soaked in Sloane's Liniment which was the panacea of the age – probably because it was heavily advertised in the *Christian Herald* under the photograph of a venerably bearded gentleman who could be taken to represent Mr Sloane or the Lord, depending on one's imagination and credulity. But I would have none of it, because I knew from my own experience, and that of others, that if I missed a couple of days of school Miss Dalbeith would leather me on two counts – firstly for being absent at all, and secondly for daring to contract a cold in flagrant breach of her credo that gaping windows and draughts of snell Atlantic air were antidotal to everything from sneezles to measles. To be absent for a month was acceptable, because it might presage the onset of T.B. which was still the scourge of our society, and, in any case, a prolonged absence necessitated a certificate from the doctor or the nurse and not even Miss Dalbeith would fly in the face of one of those.

With hindsight and the mellowing of the years it is becoming more possible to concede that much of Miss Dalbeith's preoccupation with fresh air and hygiene may have stemmed from a deep-rooted fear. Our people had come to accept tuberculosis (or consumption as it was more commonly called) as one of the awesome hazards of life in much the same way, I suppose, as people in parts of India or Africa accepted leprosy as endemic or even maledictory. To 'end up in the sanatorium' was a terrible threat to hang over one person out of every three, but that was only a statistical rationalization of the situation. In the reality it was worse. When tuberculosis struck a family, living in the smoky, clammy, confines of an airless thatched house, it wasn't just the one member it claimed – over the years it could creep its insidious way through the family, picking off its victims in completely unpredictable order. It was a fearsome social blight, and the efforts to combat it were pathetic. In some areas of the island, a patient fortunate enough to be released from the sanatorium after treatment was often lodged in a shack away from the rest of the family and was condemned to spend years, if not the rest of his life, in virtual isolation. By the same token, families with an afflicted member would find their homes shunned by neighbours fearful of infection. Nobody could have foreseen then that, even within the lifetimes of those already middle-aged, the whole plague was to be eradicated from the British scene almost overnight. And only those of us who remember the magnificently orchestrated campaign of 1952 can appreciate the miracle of the erasure of the most dreaded definition of the word 'consumption'.

Our village was almost free of the disease by sheer virtue of the fact that most of the houses were new and, consequently, built to much higher standards of hygiene, even though interior plumbing was mostly not considered necessary; they were, after all, only meant to be temporary. But the shadow still hung over us, and it must have been even more menacing for somebody like Miss Dalbeith whose education would have made her more conscious of its danger; besides she was, manifestly, a fitness fanatic anyway. Probably the very idea of being cooped up for eight hours a day in the same room as thirteen potential carriers of disease was enough to give her nightmares, and would explain why, whenever she found the slightest excuse, she conducted classes out-doors. Hebridean weather didn't always abet her and, for her own sake presumably rather than for ours, she didn't usually take us out on days as inclement as that day of Wee Barabel's funeral. But that day, out we were sent – with instructions to wipe the seats dry of snow before we sat down!

I don't know how long we had been outside before my father, muffled to his chin, came trudging along the road on his way to the cemetery. I can see him still – stopping dead in his tracks at the playground wall with disbelief writ large over what one could see of his face. 'Miss Dalbeith!' he called, with an unusual edge to his voice, and without a trace of 'please' or 'excuse me'. We couldn't hear what he said to her when she went over to the wall but, whatever it was, she seemed to take it in amiable part; and she was still smiling as she came back to us and began to give one or other of the pupils some instructions till my father had turned the corner on the way to the churchyard. She turned to me then and the ice in her voice was as chill as the snow on the ground.

'Your father says you shouldn't be outside in the cold. Come inside and I'll give you something to warm you up!'

I understood the words, although I didn't appreciate what she meant. But the oldest boy present did. And, doubtless fortified by the knowledge that he was due to leave school forever at the end of term, he stood up and began to remonstrate on my behalf. Unfortunately, for him and for me, he suffered from an affliction which the late Patrick Campbell has since made respectable on television, and before he could get out the 'P-p-p-please . . .' of 'Please Miss . . .', he was ordered inside too.

I got four of the belt, and he got six of what was known as 'cross hands'. The latter was a method in which the back of one upward-facing hand was supported on the palm of the other, with the right and left being alternated on each command of 'Change over', so that the recipient of the punishment received the maximum amount of pain from the impact of leather on flesh, and the donor achieved the max-

113

imum satisfaction. We were then ordered back outside with the assurance 'Nobody will tell me how to run my school!'

Since in our neck of the woods anything remotely connected with the mills of God ground more slowly than elsewhere, it must have been quite a while before the men returned from the burial ground. This time they were in a group. Six of them had fought the Kaiser, and one had fought Kruger as well. And even those who hadn't fought at all had heard of the Geneva Convention. They all stopped at the playground wall and leant over it in a line, looking for all the world like an unarmed firing squad; and it was obvious to the least bilingual of us that Miss Dalbeith was not being treated to Hebridean banalities about the weather. The long and the short of it was that she dismissed school for the day, and went inside and marked us all *absent*.

Our house was, at that time, the nearest occupied house of the new village to the school, and the men all solemnly turned into our gateway and into the house where my mother had already laid out the customary spread of scones and oatcakes and crowdie and cream, knowing that some of those who had furthest to walk would call in on their way home from the funeral. But she couldn't possibly have expected the whole crowd. It must have been clear to her that there was something afoot and, using my cold as a pretext, she bundled me off to bed where I promptly propped myself up with my ear against the partition. The discussion was, as I had suspected it would be, about Miss Dalbeith, and I revelled in the sentiments expressed with liberal sprinklings of words that had been invented at Vimy Ridge or Mons or Wipers (as it was called) in flagrant disobedience of the third commandment that the Lord had given to Moses on Mount Sinai.

But soon the voices began to blur, coming back to me only now and again as if from a great distance and in a great confusion. And I slipped into an oblivion out of which I didn't emerge till my mother's gentle coaxing brought me back to a hazy consciousness sometime during the next

114

morning. Apparently the nurse had been called during the night and had diagnosed measles, and I was told that the landlord had kindly arranged to lend his car and his chauffeur so that I could be evacuated north to my grandfather's in the hope that my brother and sundry others would not be contaminated. It didn't cross my mind to wonder how the landlord, who, except for a few weeks of the shooting season, spent all of his time in his native Huddersfield, could have been made privy to my incapacity, far less why he should have responded so helpfully and so uncharacteristically. It didn't matter. It was thrilling to be going for a ride in his car with his chauffeur – a local man who would have been popular anyway even if he hadn't made free with his master's car in the service of the community from the time that the latter boarded the ferry to the mainland till he came back again.

I didn't have measles. I had scarlet fever followed by various complications which resulted in a long, long stay with my grandparents. And by the time I returned to the village and to school – glory be! – Miss Dalbeith had disappeared. She had been, in the jargon of the Civil Service, *transferred* to a certain remote island in the Inner Hebrides which is now – and I make no comment – a Nature Reserve. In her place had come the woman with whom I was to achieve my seven years of 'perfect attendance'. She had a tawse – oh yes, that was, till very recently, part of the impedimenta of the Scottish school teacher – but she used it sparingly and wisely, and the leather was soft. Which was why one of the wits who read English magazines dubbed it her chastity belt.

I wish I could remember more about the circumstances surrounding the arrival of the new teacher whose name is still revered by all who sat under her, but, at the same time, the village took another step forward in its development.

'The Duchess' opened a shop.

'The Duchess' was Molly's mother who had shared the schoolhouse with us during the year of the dandelions. It was only recently that I discovered that she had, somewhat

115

tortuously, inherited the nickname either because her father had been in the service of a duke, or else, according to other sources, his father had been rather ruthless in the acquisition of land during some of the earlier land troubles. I had always thought that the name was a result of that certain air of imperiousness which, seemingly, one has to assume when one becomes head of a precarious trading enterprise, be it the British Steel Corporation or the village shop. And certainly, if the Duchess hadn't already had a slight 'cut-above-the-rest' kind of mien, she would have had to acquire it on being thrust into a situation of charging her neighbours money for things like bread and tea which she had been in the custom of serving them free at her own fireside. And to survive in business at all, she had to learn where to draw the line in the matter of 'tick' in a community which had to depend, to a certain extent, on credit facilities in between the sale of one tweed and another on the doubtful markets of the early thirties, or between the equally unpredictable incomes from the sales of heifers or tups. She was also quickly forced to learn that she must handle the business alone and unaided; her husband, the Boer War veteran, had one of the biggest hearts I've ever come across in any man, and, given an hour unsupervised, he would have given away the entire contents of the shop for free.

I remember the Duchess with affection for many reasons, but for two in particular. It became one of my more pleasant chores to walk, or run, the two miles to her shop for messages (a much nicer word than the English 'shopping') and occasionally I would be rewarded with a halfpenny or a penny for myself. On a 'halfpenny day' I would invest in Toffee Cow which had that picture of the Highland cow on the wrapper – so named I suspect because it enshrined the sweetness of temperament and the toughness of character of that famous breed of cattle. Apart from the odd occasion, like the night of James's *reiteach*, I hadn't had great experience of Toffee Cow but, with my own halfpennies, I began to develop an inordinate taste for it. It was difficult to get one's teeth into a hunk of it, and, once in, it was even more difficult to separate upper and lower jaws with the result that one could only surrender to a delicious period of succulent lock-jaw. That was a good thing when the value of a sweet was judged by its lasting quality.

Recently I came across what used to be a halfpenny bar of Toffee Cow in my local tobacco shop and, grudgingly, I invested eight pence in it for old times' sake. But, alas and alack, teeth ain't what they used to be, and I decided not to bite too hard on an old memory!

On a 'penny day' the option was much more sophisticated. The Duchess did a good line in square, creamy, toffees which she sold at a dozen for a penny, and although financial stringency ensured that they could never do my teeth or my waistline much harm, they certainly damaged my arithmetic because I grew up to believe that a dozen was thirteen.

'To him that hath shall be given', is one of the truisms of Holy Writ, and, by virtue of having the only shop, the Duchess was, in due course, allocated the sub-post-office, and, by virtue of having the sub-post-office she was later still given the Telephone Exchange of which she herself was the sole operator. It wasn't a very onerous duty because there was only one other telephone in the village in those days, and that was the one in the landlord's house which had to be routed through the Duchess. Had she happened to be curious, she could have kept check on all the movements of the landlord and his family when they were in residence, and kept the village informed on whether he or his gamekeeper was liable to be in the vicinity of the salmon river on a given night. I was too young to take an interest in the catching of salmon then, but I enjoyed the taste of it fine . . .

It was with the Duchess that I listened on a telephone for the first time. I was in the shop when the bell tinkled and she 'shushed' me and gently picked up the receiver. She listened for a few moments and then thrust the instrument into my hand with signals not to make a noise. The tinny, English conversation didn't mean very much to me because,

117

although I had mastered the first principles of the language, I found a Huddersfield accent hard to understand. But it was fascinating listening to the metallic disembodied voices. When the conversation was over I signalled to her and she replaced the telephone on its hook, assuring me that the speakers were just engineers testing the line and that there was no law against listening to them. Later I was to wonder how, in those pre-liberation days, one of the engineers came to be a female, just as, at the time, I wondered what kind of new English word 'dahling' was.

The Duchess was a very well-informed person, probably because she also retailed the first newspapers to come directly to the village. For the first while we had been dependent for such newspapers as we saw on those sent second-hand by friends, or on the *Weekly Scotsman* which my father got from Edinburgh by post. But now we were getting into the mainstream and, via the Duchess, we were getting the daily papers in pairs two days after publication. Our ex-servicemen were avid readers of them because there were rumblings of wars in places like Russia and Japan and Spain. And we, of the younger generation, tottering into literacy, were becoming members of the army of the followers of Rupert Bear. Yes! Lord Beaverbrook was seeking to further his fortunes in Scaristavore. But he reckoned without the Duchess.

The *Daily Express* expansion plans were very simple, and based on a system of 'sale or return'. But, to save the cumbersome business of parcellage and postage it was sufficient for the retailer to cut out the serial number on the front page of the unsold copies of the paper, and send the serial clippings back to Glasgow once a week, and be credited with X numbers of papers unsold. The rules said 'unsold', not 'unread', and the villagers, co-operative by nature, each took a copy of the *Daily Express* and, in due course, returned the serial number to the shop. The only person who could not be expected to co-operate was the minister's widow whose allegiance to one Lord inhibited her from defrauding another. Fleet Street must have rated our village low on the literacy charts. But it wasn't so. And it was becoming less so as the new teacher got into her stride.

I am sometimes asked why a village which started off with such promise and such optimism should have failed to burgeon and thrive and grow as it should have done. And I have to answer that one reason was the new teacher, Miss Martin. She commanded a deep loyalty, and, in the raggle-taggle clutch of 'scholars', devoid of morale, left behind by her predecessor, she instilled an extraordinary team spirit. Without realizing the consequences, she infused in all of us, to some degree or other, a passion for education, and education meant advancement, and advancement meant going away. That decreed that virtually all of the new generation, the ones who should have been the second growth of the village, left not only the village but the island. It wasn't, of course, an isolated instance of the problem, but it was acute in its microcosm in our little patch of the Highlands.

Miss Martin was a very devout woman, belonging to what is often thought of as one of the narrower and more fundamental sects of the Presbyterian Church. She was a good woman, which is sometimes a better thing to be than overly devout, but she was not above bending the rules, and bending them in such a way that those who made and administered the rules never even suspected. One of the first of her Herculean labours was to convince the Authorities in Inverness that she could raise the new village school out of the doldrums in which Miss Dalbeith had left it. And here, she was ably abetted by the Duchess and her telephone.

As soon as Inverness decided to send one of His Majesty's Inspectors of Schools on a 'surprise' tour of his constituency, a note would reach our teacher telling her that he had boarded a certain train, and by the time he had reached Kyle of Lochalsh to cross the Minch Miss Martin had been briefed on every school that he had visited, and on the questions he had asked in each one of them. The result was that, by the time he reached us, we were being prompted *not* to give the right answer before the Inspector had finished asking a question, lest we give the show away, and, here and there, ever so discreetly, a wrong answer would be planted lest we should all appear to be pedigree Mensa. Thus, rapidly, our teacher put herself into a position of strength whereby she could obtain from H.Q., without query, everything extra that she needed in the way of educational aids and equipment before settling down to the serious business of training us for the County Bursary Examinations which, by the age of eleven or twelve, would be our passports to our futures. And her God must have forgiven her her little manipulations of destiny, as He must also have forgiven the Duchess for any 'accidental taps' of the phone.

I have beside me a copy of an entry made by an Inspector in the School Log after one such 'surprise' visit. It reads thus:

Not only are the students in this school extremely versed in the three R's as we call them nowadays, but they have answered all my questions with self-confidence and a rare sense of humour. I may, perhaps, indulge myself to the extent of quoting one example of this humour, since it is a quality hitherto unassociated with this particular school. When I asked one boy a question which I intended as a jest – i.e. 'What is better than one plate of porridge?' he hesitated for a moment only, and then replied with a beguiling twinkle, 'Two plates of porridge, sir.' I have given the school a half day's holiday.

I was to get to know that Inspector well in later years when he was a venerable and highly honoured member of the Education Establishment. I hadn't seen that report of his then. Even if I had, I wouldn't perhaps have spoilt things by confessing to him that my hesitation was due to stark terror at his sudden switch from the scheduled questioning, and that the twinkle, as he called it, was relief when the teacher, standing behind him, held up two of her fingers behind his head!

Chapter Twelve

Time as it is lived doesn't slide into neat compartments, least of all in the long memory. The diarist or the historian or the biographer may be forced to define his parameters and affix his tags of time and date, and by doing so achieve an accuracy which is a different thing altogether from the truth, just as the photographer, freezing his bit of landscape, can only hope to capture a view while letting the scenery escape. And so, even if I were of a mind to do so, I could not hope to catalogue the building of the village stone by stone, because it wasn't of stones alone that it was built, but of moments, of moods, of happenings that were sometimes long and sometimes short and frequently overlapping; most indefinably of all, it was built on tears and laughter.

The sudden death of Gillespie's young sister is only remembered because of a grown man sobbing as he came to the door in the night looking for a thing called help, which he couldn't define, and which couldn't, with all the warm will in the world, be given him except in tears and platitudes. I won't even recognize her if I meet her in a Great Beyond, and yet it had been a glimpse of her naked body while we were playing one day that had first flashed into my consciousness the difference between boys and girls, and dispelled forever the puzzlement of procreation without destroying the mystery. It would be senseless to put a date or time on such a legacy. But her death was a stitch in the tapestry of our community because her father, who had been the singer of the village, never sang a Gaelic song again.

But nothing else stopped. The clover still ripened before the corn, and the autumns still followed the summers. The years were just the times we lived in, and it is successive generations that have called them 'The Thirties' and given them labels like 'hungry' and 'angry' and the rest of it. We who lived in them hadn't learnt not to be optimistic. But slowly, and behind the rest of the country, the Depression was beginning to reach out to us. Two or three of the crofters had been able to take advantage of the Government's 'Grant and Loan' scheme, and move out of their temporary shacks into grand new stone houses with two spacious rooms downstairs, and two bedrooms and a closet upstairs and, wonder of wonders, a bathroom where, as one old man put it, he was 'expected to do inside the house things for which God had provided secluded corners in the fresh air'. Suddenly, however, the 'Grant and Loan' scheme was frozen, and only one bachelor crofter was able to continue with the building of his 'white house', as the new agricultural cottages were called, and it was a mystery to people how he was able to carry on when he couldn't possibly have had any more financial resources than the rest.

The *Daily Express* was full of stories of riots and marches in Glasgow, and pictures of people queueing up at soup kitchens in cities throughout the land. But it all seemed very remote and far away, and no more immediate to us than the potted history that was beginning to be fed to us in school. The disasters of strangers are always remote, even today when television and radio bring Bangladesh and Kampuchea into our living rooms, and as children we were only vaguely aware that there was a certain sombre quality creeping into the conversations and attitudes of our parents and friends.

We were all right. By now, Daisy's first calf which, in the homely and meaningless little tradition, had been given to me and left to me to name, was now in calf herself. Unlike her mother who was pure black, she was almost white with black patches, and, with great originality, I had christened her Spotty. I have never been able to puzzle out why our domestic animals were always given English names. The village was full of Rosies, and Pansies and Slippers and nobody seemed to find anything incongruous in a red, broad-shouldered Highland stirk, with a menacing mane flopping over his beady eyes, being called Brasso after a popular metal polish. Our own menagerie consisted of Daisy and Spotty, and a Rosy who was Spotty's half-sister; the sheepdog Fanny had been sired by Grandfather's Pharaoh; the Persian cat which came after Great Aunt Rachel's victim was called Tiger; the bottle-fed lamb, which grew into a hefty ewe and haunted the doorstep for years in search of tid-bits even when she had lambs of her own at foot, was called Betsy. Poor Betsy! She slipped on the ice and broke her leg one winter, and we ate her without a qualm.

I can only assume that the yen for English names for the beasts was merely because people revelled in the freedom of being able to call them what they chose, instead of being hamstrung by the immutable tradition which decreed that children had to be named, in strict rotation, after relatives from alternating sides of the parenthood even where, as often happened, that resulted in there being three Donalds in the one family, or two Johns, or a Mary Kate, a Mary Effie, and a Mary Jean. It was a tradition which led to absurd situations in cases where, for example, a John, called 'Big John' by virtue of being the first born, turned out to be a five foot nonentity, while his younger brother, Little John, grew into a six-footer with shoulders like a bull.

Anyway, the accouchement of Spotty was awaited with great excitement, because this was going to be the first calf that we could rear for sale. I remember it well, because I was allowed to sit up into the early morning to await her delivery. Being a first calf, one couldn't be certain how the mother would react, and, in any case, an extra pair of hands would come in useful to hold the lantern and help clean the little newcomer and lift him into the straw-lined cage that had been prepared for him. There was also the fact that I had slim hands and was already expert in turning lambs threatening a breech delivery. Although such a feat would be beyond my strength in the case of a calf so positioned, I could, at the very least, help ease his head through without damage to the mother's vulva if he happened to be one of those awkward ones with stumps of horns developed in the womb or had the umbilical cord wrapped round his neck. Crofter boys had to learn how to deal with such exigencies in those days when we had no access to vets.

I always felt very important on the rare occasions when, for some reason or other, I was allowed to sit up late alone with father. They were few and far between. Sometimes it was when a storm was blowing and he would keep watch in case a haystack threatened to blow away; occasionally if there was a serious illness in the village he would delay going to bed lest somebody come for assistance; once or twice a year it was to await a new calf. He was at his relaxed best then and always spoke to me as if I were an adult. He would explain an item from the newspaper, or he would discuss some aspect of village life; but, sooner or later, the subject would turn to my future, and, without undue hectoring or admonition, he would enlarge on the benefits of education and point out the many advantages I had over himself when he was my age and schooling was regarded as a frill on the edge of living. That he was well educated himself was thanks to his mother's influence (she had inherited a reverence for education from the clerics) and, later, as a result of his voracious reading. He always hinted that journalism would be a good career, and I suspect that that was what he would have liked to have done himself.

The only subject that he would not ever be drawn on was the one that I wanted most to hear about. The war. Neither with me nor with anybody else would he ever discuss it, and it was from others that I gleaned that he had been a sniper. He would never allow even a shot-gun in the house, and although he allowed me to borrow a neighbour's when

I grew older, he wouldn't let me take it into the house nor would he handle it himself. 'Your father had nine lives if ever a man had,' an old comrade of his once said to me, but he wouldn't enlarge on what he meant. And so that was all I ever got to know about that area of his life which most stirred my curiosity as an adventure loving boy.

Sometime before dawn, Spotty calved. The birth was straightforward and uncomplicated, but I'll never forget the look of bewildered disbelief on my father's face as he stared down at the limp and lifeless form lying in its gelatinous film. 'It's dead,' he said softly, automatically reaching for his pipe. 'God, that's all we needed.'

The deadly seriousness of his tone registered with me, but I didn't feel like querying it. I was too busy gritting back the tears as I automatically scraped some of the mucous off the calf's nose and held it out to Spotty to lick. I had been taught that a cow wouldn't let her milk flow until she had been allowed at least a token licking of her calf.

'Let's leave him on the dung heap till morning', my father said flatly, 'and make sure the dog doesn't get out.'

He sealed off the cord, and we carried the little black body out of the byre on the sack that we had laid over the gutter to receive him. We didn't speak again as we went into the house. Father paused to check on the fire before he blew out the lamp, and we went through to the bedroom and undressed in the dark. As I slipped in beside my brother I heard my mother stirring and whispering 'Male or female?'

'Male,' he replied, not bothering to lower his voice. 'Still-born.'

'Oh, no!' Again the extreme concern in the voice was noticeable, but I buried my head in the pillow and sobbed myself to sleep. I had come across stillborn lambs by the dozen. I had killed rabbits. I had drowned pups and kittens. But there was something new and awful about a big, sinewy, dead calf.

'John! Finlay! One of you! Come here quick! Both of you! Quick!'

125

I was still half asleep as I collided with my father in the bedroom door.

'What the hell's the matter?'

My father rarely used an expletive, but I think he thought my mother had had a seizure or been attacked by one of the cows as he looked at her leaning, gasping, against the door-post with her hair uncoiled over her shoulders and the empty milk pail in her hand.

'The c-calf!' She spluttered. 'He's at the end of the house!'

By the grace of God there were no neighbours around as my father and I padded into the muddy, bitter morning in our shirt tails. Not that it mattered. If one were to believe the song that Gillespie's mother composed later, the whole village was out and beheld us in unmentionable detail. Gaelic poetic humour is capable of ribaldry that, in English, would be deemed coarse beyond measure!

What mattered at the time was that, there, standing splay-legged, wide-eyed and shivering, was an angular black calf, looking bemused as if he had come from another world. Which, come to think of it, he probably had.

He had been no trouble to carry out to the dung heap a few hours earlier, but now, active and gangling and slippery, it was all that the three of us could do to get him back to the byre and into his cage. Whatever psychological effect his experiences may have had on him, his lungs were unimpaired, and, in no time at all, he had his mother and the other two cows bellowing in response. They raised a sympathetic echo which spread from byre to byre till the township sounded like a festival of bassoons.

'Hurry back to the house before anybody sees you. I'll give him some of his mother's milk and he'll be fine.' My mother had recovered her composure, and was now trying to con-trol her smile, knowing full well that a man in his shirt tails is spare of a sense of humour at the best of times, even more so when he's up to his naked ankles in the muck on the floor of a byre. I knew better than to say anything as I sat waiting for my father to finish with the basin so that I could wash my own feet.

It was early evening before he made any reference to the subject. Mother had just come in from her third milking of Spotty and we were all sitting round the table having a supper of beestings.

'I'll have the naming of this calf', he said, looking at me with the tell-tale muscle in his jaw twitching.

'What?' I asked.

'Lazarus.'

And so it came to pass that Spotty's firstborn was Lazarus. And if I hadn't remembered Lazarus just now, I would have forgotten what a treat 'beestings' was in the relative monotony of our diet; it is a delicacy fast going out of existence, like crowdie and cream itself, as the domestic cow disappears, and the impersonal vans with their crates of milk slip through the villages, furtively, in the mornings.

The second and third batches of milk that come from a cow after calving are the best for beestings. The first milking is syrupy thick and yellow and it was always fed to the calf to get his digestive system going. And there was, usually, just enough to feed the calf. But, by the second milking, the cow was giving far more than the calf could cope with, and the milk still had a strong thickish quality which continued into the third or even the fourth day. This was beestings. And when the milk, at that stage, was heated, it turned into something resembling granular curds and whey, but with a far stronger flavour. It was claimed to be very nourishing, and a plate of it was a meal in itself.

It was only for one season that we had three cows, because they proved to be more than we could house, and harvest for, and more than my mother could milk. Had there been any co-operative type planning of our agriculture, things could have been so organized that a croft like ours could have been the milk supplier for the township, while others might have concentrated on the specialities for which they were best fitted, be that the production of vegetables, or cattle feed, or wool or mutton. On the face of it there is no reason why Harris mutton should not be as highly prized and marketable a commodity as Harris Tweed. But the crofter was, by his very nature an individualist, and though, in times of trouble or of need he would share out his last handful of meal or his last bag of potatoes, his philosophy was one of self-sufficiency and independence. A philosophy, however, is rarely a substitute for a policy.

Two cows were judged to be the manageable ideal for a family. One could be kept farrow for a year to supply milk in the winter while the other was in calf, then their roles alternated. A cow like Daisy, who was a superb milker in her prime, could produce four gallons of milk a day when the machair grazing was at its most lush in summer. And the variety of food forms into which that milk could be converted was almost endless. First there was, of course, the milk itself for drinking. The balance was set out in large flat basins to yield enough cream to keep the family in fresh butter for immediate use, leaving pounds over each week for salting for winter. Once the cream had been removed, gallons of thick, sour milk were left over each week, and the sour milk, when it was stood on a warm fire, converted into crowdie (or cottage cheese as it's now called) which floated to the surface of tangy, refreshing whey – the ideal drink for hot days of peat-cutting or hay-making. Some crowdie was used fresh, while the bulk of it was salted and put into heavy presses lined with muslin, where it matured into kebbucks of cheddar which would store indefinitely. But the greatest delicacy of them all was the crumbly crowdie mixed with fresh cream which, piled high on a fresh oatcake spread with fresh butter combined into a flavour with an inbuilt memory. Crowdie and cream! The bitter and the sweet blending as they so often do, in an experience for which there isn't one single word that I know of, whether relishing the dream or the reality.

We didn't dream for long, or else we dreamt too much. The revival of Lazarus was not a portent of good days ahead, romantic as the notion could be made to seem if truth didn't dictate otherwise. Although I didn't know it at the time, my father's distress, echoed in my mother's whispered 'Oh, no!' at the news of the stillborn calf was not just the normal

128

reaction of the farmer or crofter to the loss of an item of stock. We were to lose many beasts over the years and I was to hear their losses bemoaned, but no response of my parents was to impinge so sharply on my subconscious as that one. Much later I was to understand why. Before he was born, the calf had been earmarked for sale as a stirk, and he represented the next year's rent. Without realizing it, we were moving further and further into a money economy, and we were doing so at a time when that economy was in desperate recession in the rest of the world.

Unbeknownst to us, things that had been luxuries, like Glasgow bread, tinned meats, bacon, jams, and countless other things that I can't even isolate now because they're such mundane items on every shopping list, were, suddenly, no longer luxuries but necessities. Our main source of hard cash had always been the tweeds that my mother spun and which (till such time as we got our own loom) were woven for her for free by my grandfather on father's side who was a handloom weaver by trade. Our sheep-stock hadn't built up sufficiently for us to be able to sell many lambs without depleting the source of our wool for tweeds. The circle was closing into a vicious one.

Slowly the mainland markets for tweeds dried up as the textile industry throughout the country ran into difficulty, and we were forced back on the local merchants who – sometimes ruthlessly and sometimes because they were in trouble themselves – exploited the situation by buying at rockbottom prices and, gradually, by not buying at all except on a barter system whereby they would take a tweed at a nominal price of half-a-crown (twelve and a half pence) a yard, and refund its value in groceries over a period of weeks. If the merchant could hold out till times improved he was bound to make a killing because he was trading in in wholesale terms, and selling at full retail profit. It was inevitable that human greed – the quality as hackneyed as the phrase – would evince itself, and some merchants soon became notorious for 'having a broad thumb'. They were the ones who would go to the length of counting their own thumb in with the yardstick when they were measuring a tweed for purchase, and the web of tweed which a woman had measured as forty-five yards on her own kitchen table, could well be forty-three on the merchant's counter. Having been lucky enough to get a lift to the shop in Calum the Post's van, she would be unlikely to face up to the prospect of humping the tweed back home on her back even though those two yards represented the loss of a goodly part of a week's necessities.

Steadily, matters got worse. There was a limit to the amount of tweed that even the best intentioned merchant could afford or risk to stock-pile, and the women, since it was they who were in the front line when it came to shopping, were increasingly forced to plead for 'tick' against the day when 'things would get better' as they surely must. That was where poverty ended, and humiliation began. In a society where credit and overdrafts are an accepted and even applauded way of life, and where, sometimes, the bigger the debt the greater the credibility, it is hard to imagine the degradation of a woman with a hole in her shoe begging for a quarter pound of tea and a pound of sugar 'till next week', as if the world was going to change in seven days.

Worst of all was the dread of 'going on the parish'. It was an old phrase for a current phenomenon. Times have changed in that respect too, and the phrase 'social security' isn't even a euphemism – it's an honourable description of an entitlement, and it is, by and large, anonymous. But, in a small community which had started off with high hopes and pride, 'going on the parish' was all the more degrading because the arbiter of need was, invariably, someone who had once been a youthful equal in courtship or in play.

Charity came on Thursday. That was the day on which Calum the Post stopped at practically every door in the village and dispensed buff envelopes containing Money Orders which he invariably cashed on the spot. There were various official phrases that Calum was unable to understand, and 'Not negotiable' and 'Payee only' were two of them. I have no idea how far the dole – the blanket term for meagre state hand-outs – went. But, at the very least, it must have covered essentials like paraffin and oatmeal and the salt herring which was the keystone of our diet and which we had to buy because we couldn't fish our Atlantic shore, having nowhere remotely safe enough for anchorage.

There was, of course, no danger that we would starve. Our poverty was relative to standards which were new to our parents' generation, and it was acute only relative to their aspirations. During the winter that I went to school for several weeks on end wearing sand-shoes with no soles to them except bits of dried rabbit skin which my father had to replace every second morning, I still had a bowl of oatmeal brose for breakfast every morning, potatoes and salt herring for lunch every day and eggs in some form or other every night. And, usually, a salt mutton meal on a Sunday. It was only once that I remember hearing a strange, intermittent noise and looking up to find that it was the sound of my mother's tears sizzling on the top of the stove as she tried to manufacture some kind of oatmeal patties from the only ingredients she had in the house. I suppose I only remember it because it was dramatically unusual, and because the memory appealed to the sense of the dramatic in myself in later years.

Lazarus represented the nadir of our fortunes. When he was sold (as a yearling) at the annual cattle sale – a sale which was by then reduced to a symbolic sham – he fetched less than a pound, because any more would have made it uneconomical for a buyer to ship him to the mainland. It was that year too that we killed Daisy. She had been a mature cow when we got her, and we could no longer afford to feed her when there was no market for her progeny, and there were two other younger cows to maintain a milk supply. We needed meat, and we could deplete the sheep-stock no further. One or two of the other crofters had already killed their older cattle, and having salted as much meat as was prudent or possible had divided the remainder throughout the village. We did the same with Daisy, and my last mem-

131

ory of her is of yards of her intestines, cleaned and salted and inflated and hung to mature in the peat smoke till such time as they could be made into mealy puddings. Daisy had not only launched us on our way, she had kept us going when the way got rough, and, long after the boards had begun to show through the cheap bedroom linoleum, we had a warm cowskin rug under our feet on winter mornings.

Times of depression and recession are alleged to breed crime and prejudice, and, in urbanized communities where the pressures of proximity can throw disparities of standards into bitter relief, it may well be that the patterns of order and mutual respect can be disturbed and normally containable grievances fomented. But, in a small rural community wherein there is no real spectrum of 'haves' and 'have nots' hard times can cement relationships and strengthen foundations, and the Polonius dictum on borrowing and lending gets stood on its head. Putting aside the rapacity of a few merchants – which was forgiven as an understandable human failing anyway – only two incidents occurred that were sufficiently different from the humdrum norm to stamp themselves on the boyhood memory.

I mentioned earlier that the taking of rabbits was forbidden to us, and yet the reader must have guessed that my father couldn't very well have lined my sand-shoes with rabbit skins without inflicting a certain amount of grievous bodily harm on the original wearers of the skins. In truth, the landlord's prohibition was more honoured in the breach than in the observance, and by none more so than our cat Tiger who, true to his name, was a killer of the first order. He could take a buck rabbit twice his own size without effort, and without leaving a mark on him. But he didn't have any great flair for skinning and jointing, and the result was that, on any given morning, the first person to open the front door was liable to find four or five rabbits, still warm, laid out side by side on the front step, with Tiger patiently waiting for somebody to do the bloody work of gralloching them and feeding him the tid-bits of liver and lights. If the Reverend Dr George Macleod could see the hand of the Lord in shipwrecks of timber landing on the beach when he was rebuilding Iona Abbey, I don't see why we shouldn't see the finger of God in the claws of Tiger. But, be that as it may, we took little convincing that Tiger's ancestors must have more than justified the veneration in which they were held in the Middle East in ancient times when he began to supplement his free-will offering of rabbits with plump sea-trout. It was on a Sunday morning that my father first opened the door to find five sizeable sea-trout laid out neatly on the step, with the cat looking even more pleased with himself than usual. Some of the neighbours with whom we shared our bounty pretended not to be as surprised or puzzled as we were, and one or two who were, in most things, more worldly-wise than the rest, were able to confirm that cats were not as scared of the water as popular belief would have one accept, and they could even cite cases of cats that had been seen to hook fish out of rock pools. Nobody however could explain why Tiger should always go fishing on a Saturday night.

When news began to get round that the landlord was accusing his tenants of thieving, people just smiled and assumed that he was referring to the occasional salmon that disappeared from under his gamekeeper's nose, or the even more occasional stag that vanished from his hill. But the smiles hardened when he was heard to be accusing the locals of gaining entry to his game larder and removing the Saturday catches of his guests and himself. 'Clever buggers,' he said to my father whom he trusted, 'but stupid for all that! Beats me why they clean out the sea-trout and leave fourteen-pounders of salmon untouched!' My father could hardly explain that even a muscular cat would find it hard to get a fourteen-pound salmon through an eight-inch airing shaft. But he took extra care to see that Tiger didn't get locked in the house on a Saturday night from then on, and the neighbours accepted any slurs on their honesty with a shrug and a quizzical smile.

The second episode was a different matter altogether and, even now as I write, I cannot help hoping that the man at the heart of it is still around to read this. When the inevitable day came that even the kindliest merchant could no longer take tweeds on spec, people continued, helplessly, to search for outlets for the only marketable commodity they had. Long since, the miserable, drenching, salty scrabbling for whelks among the seashore rocks had ceased to offer its meagre reward; it now cost more to send a bag of whelks to Billingsgate than one could hope to get from its sale. But, from time to time, a rumour would reach us that a woman in some other village had managed to sell a tweed to some shop or firm in Edinburgh or Birmingham or somewhere and, immediately, there would be a slight surge of optimism and that particular shop or firm would be deluged with two-inch square samples (or patterns as they were called) of tweeds from all over Harris. Sometimes the shops replied saying 'no'. Sometimes they didn't even acknowledge the letter. Very, very rarely there would come an offer to buy – usually at a mean price; but no matter how poor the price, it still represented hard cash and as such was worth more than the barter value in the local shops. Such sales were few and far between, but they kept hope alive.

Then, one week, there appeared in the local paper an advertisement *asking* for tweeds, and offering two-and-sixpence a yard for self coloured tweeds and two-and-elevenpence a yard for checks. Samples were to be sent to a Mr Brooks in Manchester. It was incredible! Somebody was actually asking for samples. And the price was good. A wave of hope went through the township; neighbours called in the house to ask if mother had heard about the advertisement. My father remarked, rather guardedly, that things were 'maybe beginning to look up'.

My mother had two or three tweeds of different lengths stacked under a dustsheet in the bedroom, including one of which she was inordinately proud – a fifty-yard web of black and white dog-tooth or shepherd's check, hand-spun throughout from some fine wool which she had selected from the few Cross Cheviot fleeces that we had. A shopkeeper who was vaguely related to her had, rather reluctantly, agreed to buy it, but when she went to see him he was only too delighted to be released from his side of the bargain.

'Another letter for Brooks, eh?' said Calum the Post when I intercepted him with an envelope containing the standard two inches square of sample next morning. That told its own story. Calum probably had a letter from every house in the village, each single one carrying a fragment of a family's hope under its flap.

Mr Brooks was not only a selective dealer, but a courteous one into the bargain. By return post he replied to every single letter – alas, not always placing an order but, at least, regretting his lack of interest in this particular piece of tweed or that, and returning the sample with the hope that he might be in a position to do business at some future date. As far as one could make out, as the women met to commiserate or congratulate, he placed firm orders for about half the tweeds that had been put on offer, and it was clear that he had a distinct preference for fairly bold patterns and checks. He went out of his way to be complimentary about my mother's 'shepherd's check' and the tone of his letter implied that this was no casual dabbler in the market; a couple of phrases suggested that not only did he appreciate the subtle differences in quality of certain wools, weaves and finishes, but also that he was acutely aware of the flaccid state of the market at the time. There was a heady air of high spirits in the house that night. My father had been a grocer's assistant for a short time in his youth, and he always prided himself on his talent for parcelling; that evening he excelled himself as my mother teased him for creating a work of art that Mr Brooks would duly rip apart without even noticing. But he joked back that the real art of salesmanship was in the presentation of the product; his neat packaging might impress the Macdonald name on the Brooks memory more than the quality of the tweed, and when the time came for a repeat order Mr Brooks would call for 'the address of the man who makes the artistic parcels in Harris'. Long before bedtime the tweed was packaged as if it were destined for Sotheby's of London instead of Brooks of Manchester, and

135

in the morning it was taken on its way by Calum the Post, although by no stretch of the imagination could fifty yards of Harris Tweed be deemed to fall within the weight restrictions of the Royal Mail. 'The van's down on its springs with tweeds,' said Calum; 'it's just as well it's by sea and rail they're going, or the Post Office would be charging a fortune in stamps.'

Two weeks passed. And then three. Courteous letters went off to Mr Brooks. Then angry ones. But there was no reply. People unsophisticated in the complexities of trade didn't know how to proceed, and in the end they turned to the one man with whom most of them had had least dealing – the Bank Manager. There was little he could do, but it was enough. No such man as our Mr Brooks had a bank account anywhere in Manchester, nor was there any record of his existence. The address to which the tweeds had been sent was a temporary 'convenience address' and the premises had been closed and shuttered for a fortnight. And that was the end of the story. There was no point in starting any complicated proceedings for the sake of a few hundred yards of tweed of little or no current market value. Nothing had been lost except long days and evenings of effort. And a few days of hope.

I have no idea how those incidents were juxtaposed, or why they even found a compartment in the long memory which is so short on worthier counts. Probably just because the incidents extend naturally into stories. There is no story in a parcel of groceries from an aunt . . . nor in a dollar in an envelope from an uncle faring not much better in America . . . nor in a visit from the Duchess, just dropping in to rest her feet, and the finding of a quarter pound of tea on St Clement's bench after her departure . . . These were just stitches in the tapestry of the years of the Crowdie and Cream, and the touches that put the sweet in the bitter sweet.

Chapter Thirteen

Just when it seemed that the village had settled down to its final format – in as much as a community ever has a final format – its whole character was suddenly changed by the removal of the old hillside population. It was as if the old host rose were removed once the new graft had taken hold. It meant that the school roll dropped by four to the thirteen at which it was to remain static for the next five years or so. The four who left were to drop out of my ken forever as they were melded into a new school in a new village seven miles north of us.

From the earliest Clan MacLeod days, the rich tack or estate of Luskentyre had been run on the lines of a sporting estate with a large Home Farm, and occupied, consequently, by a wealthy absentee tenant landlord who required only a small number of retainers to keep the place ticking over in between salmon runs. For some reason Luskentyre had failed to find a buyer when Harris had been sold off in bits and pieces after the death of Lord Leverhulme in 1925, and the estate had remained the property of Leverhulme's trustees but leased to the wealthy Venables family from Kent. The Department of Agriculture made every effort to get the Leverhulme trustees to subdivide the land and rent it out as crofts in the same way as our landlord had been compelled to do, but trustees and tenant alike remained obdurate. At last the Department invoked its powers of compulsory purchase and threw Venables out lock, stock and barrel, refusing to leave him any land whatsoever. They left him only the fishing rights and the Big House which he abandoned and allowed to go to rack and ruin.

Luskentyre was probably a better agricultural proposition than our area, but the farming side of the estate had been allowed to deteriorate in favour of sport, so that by the time the Department of Agriculture acquired it, it was virtually over-run by rabbits. The new superiors estimated that it could be made to carry eighty cattle and five hundred sheep, and, on that basis, they divided it into ten crofts of which the Black Shepherd and his fellow cottars were given one each. Thus, at last, they got their long-awaited reward for their raiding, their imprisonment and their patience, but a lot of the colour went out of our fragile society when they left.

In some ways they got a better deal than we did, because they were the direct tenants of the Department of Agriculture, with no other landlord in between. While we had the umbrella of the Department and its guarantees for the security of our tenure, we still had an immediate private Landlord who had been allowed to retain a sizeable farm for himself and a certain superiority over us. For example, he regarded rabbits, which were the plague of our early existence, as Game, and, instead of taking steps to suppress them, he introduced a strain of black Dutch rabbit to strengthen the breed and make them better sport. Even when they scourged our crops we were not, officially, allowed to trap or shoot or snare them. It was a nice challenge for growing boys!

I reckon that, in the early thirties, we were lapping a full decade behind even the most faintly urbanized areas of the mainland in terms of the most rudimentary social amenities, although by no means so in terms of attitudes of quality of life. The town of Stornoway still didn't have a communal electricity supply, and we hadn't even graduated to the vapourized Tilly lamp whose crisp white light was soon to replace the mellower glow of the double-wick paraffin lamp; the Tilly may have been easier on the

138

reading eye, but its spartan brass and chrome lines never developed into an art form to touch the ornate, fluted, outlines of tinted glass and lacquered pedestals that gave character to the Victorian oil lamp. It was by the light of one of them that I graduated slowly and painfully from the drudgery of the Home Reader to the peripatetic adventures of Rupert Bear in a world which was strangely real, and the world of Dixon Hawke which was not. In London, the British Broadcasting Corporation was taking over the development of television from the Baird Company long before the first wireless set reached our village, and the nearest we had to 'provided' entertainment was my father's square oak box of a gramophone with a large green horn, with a picture of a dog of indeterminate pedigree listening to a square oak gramophone with a large green horn, on which there was a picture of a dog of indeterminate pedigree listening. . . .

The selection of records was limited to a dozen or so Gaelic singers, who were famous in their time, giving renditions of simple folk-songs in ornate, stylized Victorian settings, and two or three Harry Lauder pieces. Sometimes, of a still evening, my father would open the window and push the horn out through it in the hope that it would entice one or two of the younger neighbours to come in. And sometimes they would. And the evening would develop into a story-telling session during which my mother would sit spinning late into the night, leaving the spinning wheel only to replenish the tea-pot. My brother and I would sit quietly listening, careful not to draw attention to ourselves, but, sooner or later we were hustled off the bed. It didn't matter much. We just sat hunched in bed with our ears to the partition, hoping to hear things that we weren't supposed to hear, till sleep overcame us. But such evenings were few and far between. There weren't many visitors to go round, and it was a special occasion when somebody from one of the neighbouring villages decided to make a pilgrimage on his bicycle and drop in unannounced. There was a time when

139

we could have depended on James to arrive fairly frequently, but, shortly after his marriage, he decided that he couldn't make ends meet just by working on his father's croft, and he went back to sea. Instead of being sorry to see him go, people were pleased for him and spoke about how fortunate he was to know a skipper who was able to offer him a berth in 'these difficult times'.

The recession of the thirties did not seem, materially, to affect the education system as much as national crises do now. Certainly not as far as our village was concerned. It may be that the new teacher had acquired so much muscle with the Education Authority that the members of its various committees, who were then, as now, chosen for their spare time rather than their talents, were unable to gainsay her merest request. Or it may be that wise men with abaci, having computed that the population of the world had reached two billion, were confident that a spillover of the international trend would be evidenced in Scaristavore sooner or later, and that the current stability of the population owed more to good luck than to continence. For whatever reason, there was a sudden descent on the school of joiners and slaters and plumbers, and, without any apparent disruption of the curriculum, we found the building being transformed around us.

It soon became obvious that however little else they had in common, Miss Martin and Miss Dalbeith shared a passion for hygiene. But where the old teacher had been content with punishing us for not sharing her enthusiasm, the new one was determined that we should accept as an article of faith that cleanliness was next to Godliness, and when the green and yellow walls were repainted in the same colours, of which Inverness County Council obviously had limitless supplies, she had a framed motto to that effect hung up in place of the semi-nude harvesters of rice. To ensure that we had the facilities with which to practise the new faith, the dim passage-way that led from the front door to the schoolroom, and had hitherto been furnished only with variously elevated cloakroom pegs, was now brightly lit by a brand new window, and fitted out with wash-hand basins with brass taps that gushed running water. The 'wee houses' at the back, which had been used as lumber dumps for as long as anybody could remember, were cleared and equipped with chemical toilets that tainted the air with a smell less acceptable by far than that which it was supposed to combat. The phrase 'Please miss, I want out' was amended to 'Please miss, may I go to the toilet?' and the idea was that, having been, one then underlined one's mission for the whole school by ostentatiously running cascades of water over one's hands in the cloakroom. The theory was fine, but the end result was that we just refused to ask out, and when the intervals were called the boys made a mad dash to vault over the playground wall and line up against the back of it in the time-honoured fashion. For the girls it must have been excruciatingly embarrassing. They tried to adopt the genteel fashion, but after a few of them had looked up from the crouch to find two sets of grubby male fingers hooked over the top of the door, and two pairs of boggling eyes staring down through the gap below the lintel, they abandoned all pretence of sophistication and reverted to slinking off to the sand dunes, now much more self-consciously and conspicuously than before.

The major transformation – which also had its hygienic associations – came with the disappearance of the five-seater desks. They vanished without warning in the course of one weekend, taking with them whole genealogies in the form of hundreds of initials that had been surreptitiously carved on them by successive generations since 1892. They were replaced by smart two-seater desks, graded in size, each with a locker under a hinged lid. They had no slots in the top. The old germ-laden slates, which had been scratched on and spat on by our predecessors and ourselves, disappeared forever, and the word 'jotter' was added to our growing vocabulary. It was a treacherous, betraying thing, the jotter. No longer could a quick lick and a slick with the finger eliminate a mistake when one glimpsed the correct answer on a neighbour's slate; with the jotter one had to go through the whole tell-tale gamut of stroking out, which was frowned on anyway, or else hope to procure a rubber without drawing too much attention to one's purpose. The abolition of the slate at least lessened the wear and tear on the jersey sleeve, releasing it briefly, for its secondary purpose. One of the very first jotter pages that I ever laboriously filled was 'I must not wipe my nose on my sleeve', only to have to do it all over again. But at least I never forgot again how to spell sleeve!

Gillespie and I shared one of the new two-seater desks, and I suppose it afforded us our first little sensation of relative privacy. We fixed an imaginary line down the middle of the locker, and we came to an agreement that each would housekeep his own side of the line and respect any bits of private property that one or the other might want to store away from the prying eyes and fingers of the family at home. We also devised a system whereby two quick nudges of the bare knee led to a simultaneous lifting of the lid of the desk for a quick conference on a matter of spelling or addition; if we were caught out later with the same mistake we could swear in all honesty that we had not been 'copying', which meant, literally, looking at the other's book and was not deemed to embrace whispered consultations.

I haven't seen Gillespie these many years. Of the thirteen of us whom I have always regarded as being 'the school' because that number remained for the longest time static, Gillespie is the one who has wandered furthest afield. And, although as boys we often swore lifelong friendship as boys do, we have never met or corresponded since we had our one and only evening on the beer just about the time that we both became men. So I've never been able to ask him whether he remembers the sensation that he nearly caused . . . the time-bomb laugh that he planted . . . or whatever it is you call it when you commit a solecism which, only long years later, explodes on the consciousness of yourself and others.

There is an old Gaelic proverb which says that 'rivalry turns a township's best furrow', and it means, I suppose, that no ploughman wants to be seen to be worse at his craft than his neighbour. And rivalry, rather than any goadings or threats, was the means favoured by Miss Martin to spur us on towards an education. Nowadays, in the general frenzy to level life down rather than up, it is not considered good educational policy to create stars, lest the fellow at the tail of the class, be he lout or laggard, develops one of the fashionable complexes of which, it seems, more are being discovered every day. Occasionally our sense of competition was fanned by the promise of some small reward or other; usually it was enough to bask in the approval of the teacher. She may not have been outstandingly successful in her efforts to turn us into well groomed and manicured little ladies and gentlemen fit to grace a garden party, but she was, slowly and steadily, wearing down the contempt for education which had been inculcated in us by her predecessor. We graduated gently from the interminable cats sitting on their mats to simple stories of adventure, and, almost without realizing it, a working knowledge of the English language was creeping up on us, and, with it, a patent need for more and more vocabulary.

The child in an English-speaking community absorbs his vocabulary in the everyday business of living, but even during the briefest of school intervals we reverted immediately to Gaelic, and, from the moment that the school gate closed behind us at four o'clock we didn't hear a word of English spoken unless such parents as were bilingual themselves wanted to converse about something private or otherwise unsuitable for young ears. Under the circumstances, it was astonishing that, by the time we left the village school at the ages of eleven or twelve to go in search of further education, we were reasonably fluent in what was, in every way, a foreign language. One of the teacher's most innovative ploys to widen our vocabulary was what she called 'The Word Game'. It sounded as if it was meant to be fun, and, in a way, it was. The idea was that we should go home each evening and, by any means we chose, find one new word, and come to school next morning knowing exactly what the word meant, able to spell it, and prepared to deliver at least one long sentence involving the word in such a way as to render its meaning clear to the rest of the school. At the end of each morning session the school, or such members of it as were old enough to understand words of more than three letters, would adjudicate and vote on the quality of the words, and the winner would get a red star stuck inside the cover of his or her jotter. At the end of term, a prize would be awarded to the person with the greatest number of stars.

Gillespie and I became great rivals in the Word Game. His father had a lexicon with some pages missing, and mine had a much thumbed, fat, and elderly edition of *Chambers Twentieth Century Dictionary* which he was sometimes driven to read when there was no newspaper and he felt too tired to make yet another sortie into Gibbon's *Decline and Fall*. I don't know what kind of technique Gillespie used, but I discovered fairly quickly that there was a surpassing rich goldmine of highly unusual and exotic words among the Xs, Ys and Zs, and I became expert at regaling the school with dissertations on Vertigo and Xylophone and Yapok. Come to think of it, I'm probably one of the few people around who knows what a yapok is, unless some contemporary in Scarista Public School remembers the difficulty I had in convincing Miss Martin that if yapok were rendered inadmissible just because the animal didn't abound in Harris, then, by that token, elephant and camel would have to be disallowed too. She conceded the point with some reluctance, but indicated that she, personally, would be inclined to cast her vote in future for words that might, conceivably, crop up in the occasional conversation in some part of the British Isles. Looking back on it, the whole project was fraught with danger, and the miracle of it was that the teacher didn't get her come-uppance long before that fateful morning.

Living next door as we did, Gillespie and I invariably walked to school together, and, if we hadn't picked up any family secrets to divulge to each other, the conversation would come round to the Word Game which was always the first item on the agenda after Prayers. There was no point in being secretive with each other. We would never dream of stealing each other's words. There was no need to: there were no points to be scored since each person had to define and talk about his own word anyway. On that particular morning I was rather pleased with the word I had found, and, without prompting, informed Gillespie rather pompously that it was a sure-fire winner. It was, in fact, 'Uxorious', and it meant (and presumably still means) 'excessively fond of one's wife'. His reaction was predictable.

'How many letters?'

'Eight,' I was able to tell him, at the same time secretly wishing that I had plumbed the dictionary a little further, since eight was pretty average for a good word, and Gillespie and I had frequently scored ten in our own private needle contests, despite the fact that the teacher went to constant trouble to stress that the usefulness of a word was not always commensurate with its length. I couldn't decide whether or not I had scored a hit. Gillespie went silent, and for the life of me I couldn't make up my mind whether it was his smug or his sulky expression that he was wearing.

'What's your word?' I asked.

'I won't tell you. It's better than yours!'

'Did your father not know one?' I knew that would sting.

'I didn't ask my father. We've got a dictionary too as you know fine'.

We walked for a while in silence.

'I won't tell you the word but I'll tell you what it means.

145

It's a big kind of piano that they play in churches in the town when they're singing. My father says he saw one in Portsmouth when he was in the navy. So there's such a thing, see?'

That was good enough for me, and I wished that I had consulted my own father who had a vast vocabulary of big words culled from Gibbon and Lord Macaulay. But it was too late now, and by the time we reached school I was convinced that Gillespie must have a word of inordinate length which would knock the teacher for six. Only part of my conviction was to be realized!

School always began with Morning Prayers. Not the token nod in the direction of the Almighty which seems, for the most part, to pass for Morning Prayers now, but a full dress service starting with the Lord's Prayer which we were taught to lisp from the first day that we entered school. The fact that for the first two years at least it didn't mean anything, taught as it was in English, didn't seem to matter; the assumption was, presumably, that He to whom it was being addressed knew it off by heart of old. At a lower level, of course, the constant repetition was excellent practice in the pronunciation of English. But even now it seems strange to me that it was long after I was reasonably fluent in English that I memorized the prayer in Gaelic. Come to think of it, I suppose I was being conditioned to assume that God was a native English-speaker like most of those we were taught to regard as our superiors, just as hordes of people the world over were being taught that the God for whom they were being asked to forsake their own was white and unquestionably pro-British.

The Lord's Prayer was followed by Bible reading and study, and the accent was very heavily on the Old Testament. For a long time I was firmly convinced that the genesis had taken place in Harris, and that Ararat was probably the highest peak of the mountain range separating us from Lewis. A mile or so from the village there was a stretch of marsh land which flooded completely at

146

times of heavy rain, leaving only tall bull-rushes rearing above the water. Here, surely, Pharaoh's daughter, washing herself in the river (as we did ourselves when the weather was reasonable), stumbled across the baby Moses in a wicker basket such as my Grandfather made out of willow to carry home his peat. Sometimes, now, I wonder what city children, brought up in their brick and mortar jungles relate to when they read about the miracles of creation.

Such was the concentration on the Old Testament that we could effortlessly have transferred our allegiance to the Jewish faith. But whatever good our studies of the Pentateuch did our souls, they certainly improved our English, even if, for the first few years our conversation may have had a quaint 'hast and didst' quality about it. Moreover (there I go!) those early books of the Bible provided a rare source of blood and thunder adventure for youngsters who didn't, at that stage, have access to libraries, far less bookshops. Of course, the teacher's attempts to slip over some of the more explicit chapters of Leviticus were guaranteed to send us rushing to them at the earliest clandestine moment, and since they frequently involved recourse to the dictionary I suppose they must have made contributions to our education – liguistic and otherwise.

I will skip over the torture of the Shorter Catechism, admirable though it may be as the good man's Highway Code. It was the third item in the daily Order of Service which ended, pleasantly and mercifully, with a metric psalm. Forty-five minutes or so the Religion period lasted each morning. And then it was 'Bibles away. And on with the Word Game!' I would be dipping into the realms of fiction if I were to pretend to remember which words were trundled out by the various participants that morning. But, by simple dint of checking on the fading school photograph on my desk, I can calculate that five words were produced and defined and spelt and en-sentenced before it came to Gillespie's turn. And he was second from the last immediately before me.

'Right then, Gillespie', said the teacher, 'stand up and let's hear your word.'

Gillespie shot me a quick 'wait-till-you-hear-this' kind of look and stood up. I braced myself for some multi-syllabled semanteme which would make my 'uxorious' sound like an infant's burble and totally demolish my hopes of a red star.

'Pennies,' said Gillespie as crisply as his thick Highland accent would allow.

I couldn't believe my ears. Gillespie knew as well as I did that plurals weren't allowed, and when the teacher had made the rule, she had seized her chance to explain to us what a 'plural' was. Her brow puckered.

'You know I only allow one, Gillespie', she said.

'It is one, Miss, it's not "pennies" money.' Gillespie was almost pert in his self-confidence.

'Well, it's new to me then, Gillespie,' she said, and later she must have thanked the Lord that there were no irreverent adults present to hear her. 'Tell the class what it means.'

'It's an organ, Miss,' said Gillespie.

There is such a thing as total innocence.

'Spell it.'

'P-E-N-I-S,' enunciated Gillespie triumphantly, and I breathed with relief as I counted only five letters.

Underneath the calm exterior which she normally presented in front of the school, the teacher was a very nervous person. The sudden appearance of a stranger at the door would bring a flush of red to her neck, and under any sustained emotion the red flush would suffuse her face. It was something of which, I am sure with hindsight, she was deeply conscious. That day her blush could not be appropriately described as red. The exact word for it was vermilion, the very word with which I had unhappily lost a round of the Word Game a few days earlier because I had accidentally put two 'l's' in it! She looked at the class, rustled some papers on her desk, glanced at her watch, and went through the whole classic gamut of reaction of somebody striving to regain composure. 'Thank you, Gillespie', she said. 'Dear me, I'm afraid we've taken longer than usual. That's all we've time for today.' And she called the morning interval without as much as asking Gillespie for his sentence.

Needless to say, the interval was devoted to a lengthy discussion of the incident. Nobody could quite understand what had gone wrong although it was plain that something had gone drastically amiss. And then, one of the older boys had a flash of inspiration.

'It was all your fault,' he said, rounding on Gillespie. 'You shouldn't have used that word. You know fine the teacher belongs to the Free Presbyterian Church and they think it's a sin to use an organ with the psalms!' And that was that.

It was also the end of the Word Game. And, in all those years, neither in writing nor in conversation have I found a chance to use the word 'uxorious' till now.

Chapter Fourteen

For some weeks after the fire curtain had come down on the drama of the Word Game, our vocabularies were left to expand themselves along the more orthodox guide rails laid down in *The Royal Crown Reader*, published for the English speaking schools of the Kingdom, if not the Empire, by Thomas Nelson and Sons, Ltd., of London, Edinburgh, New York, Toronto and Paris.

The Royal School Series (that was the umbrella title) consisted of two Infant Readers and six Junior School Readers, all uniformly bound in sedate dark blue covers sporting a large crown motif to remind us, presumably, that, away in the outmost Hebrides, we were still the fortunate denizens of the great power whose domains were splurged in red across the full width of the schoolroom map. The series, unamended as far as I know, served generations of 'scholars', and I have often wondered if, in faraway corners of those red splodges, future perpetrators of insurrection were having their cultures ironed out of them by means of flat banalities in, albeit, immaculate grammar. The imagination jibs at the thought of, say, Mr Robert Mugabe being made to stand up in front of his class and read aloud such gems of poetry as

> Thinks pussy, 'The ball
> That I see in the hall,
> Is the best ball of all
> That ever I saw.

150

My kittens I'll call
From the garden wall,
And we'll toss the nice ball
From paw to paw.'

or, one class further on

Dicky bird, Dicky bird whither away?
Why do you fly when I wish you to stay?
I never would harm you, if you would come
And sing me a song while you perch on my thumb.

And yet, why not? Our native culture was as remote from
that of the hub of empire as were the separate cultures of
Messrs Mugabe and Nkomo, and the grand plan was to
smoothe them all out to an acceptable uniformity.

Our teacher was a staunch upholder of the 'system' as a
result of her own indoctrination; and it was not her instinct
but her training and the policies of government at all levels,
that made her labour to hone and polish us so that we could
take our places in a society other than our own. 'If you don't
do your sums . . . If you don't learn your spelling . . . If you
don't practise your reading . . . you'll never get away from
here.' Those were the exhortations of school and home, and
nobody ever paused to think that, particularly in those days
of the hungry thirties, *here* was a damn good place to be.
With hindsight it is almost incredible that, all over the
Highlands, men who had fought to establish their right to
the land and to create new communities such as ours, were
subscribing to a system which would ensure that their sons
would seek out lives and livelihoods elsewhere.

But our schoolmistress – while having to work within the
constraints of a dubious philosophy – was too good a teacher
to accept that she could stimulate our fluency in English, far
less share the undoubted love that she had for the language
herself, by strict adherence to text books alone. The Word
Game had been successful while it lasted, and she must have
put some considerable thought into finding for it a successor
that would be relatively free of pitfalls. She came up with

151

the idea of 'Conversation'. A fairly obvious idea, admittedly, since it was with the avowed purpose of being able to converse in it that we were learning English in the first place. It was also, she explained, something in which all thirteen members of the school could participate, given an accepted principle of handicap whereby the most junior members could get away with 'I have a black dog', while the more sophisticated citizens would be expected to enlarge on the working qualities or other attributes of their dogs, black or otherwise.

We were hers to command, and those who might not be prepared to strive to please were scared to offend. And so, for the next day or two she was regaled with sagas about the village dogs which ranged from the anthropomorphic to the downright untruthful. When some exasperated soul was stung into a protestation of 'Please Miss, Jimmy MacLean is telling lies', it gave her a chance to attempt to delineate the subtle distinctions between falsehood and fiction which is not as simple as it may seem in a basically fundamentalist society. However, when it came to 'There were three dogs on top of our dog last night and my father was throwing pails of water over them', it was manifestly time for her to steer Conversation into broader channels lest she find herself foundering in the treacherous waters of farmyard sex. Already one or two of the older pupils were beginning to revel in the manipulation of the word 'bitch' without fear of reprimand. And, slowly, she began to win. Conversation became a free-ranging half hour of diverse sentences and paragraphs on divers subjects. Till, subtly, the whole village began to become involved.

In no time at all no domestic secret was safe unless parents remembered to warn their offspring not to divulge it under pain of dire punishment. Even then, from time to time, subjects were aired in Conversation which would not normally be the subject of public discussion. For parents it must have been like living under a permanent cloud of censorship, and the end-result was an unexpected and unprecedented involvement of parents in the education of their children, and the least bed-time whisper of 'I haven't got a conversation for tomorrow' was enough to send them on a frenetic search for a subject that could be guaranteed to be innocuous. On occasion mothers and fathers found it more prudent to frame and rehearse sentences themselves, though by so doing they were laying their own syntax and grammar on the line for dissection in class on the morrow. But that was safer than having their private worlds unveiled, and I have always fancied that Conversation, to some extent or other, led to an upgrading of the English of the entire community, since lapses in the King's English could not be overlooked just on the strength of a plea of 'Please Miss, that's how my father says it.'

My own father, having had a minor difficulty with the rent publicly aired, got round the problem very neatly by ordaining that each of my Conversations must start with the words 'I read in the newspaper . . .', thus, by his way of it, killing two birds with the one stone – relieving himself of the responsibility of providing me with a topic, and ensuring at the same time that, to some extent, I actually read a newspaper. I didn't always remember to do so, of course, and frequently had to fall back on my imagination, with the result that Lord Beaverbrook would have been astounded had he heard some of the news items that were being attributed to his journalists. But at least the family's private affairs were safeguarded since even I couldn't dress them up sufficiently to make them attributable to the *Daily Express*.

But not every pupil was as effectively muzzled as I was, and domestic gossip still featured prominently in the morning news sessions. And just as I was prepared to improvise on the news from Fleet Street so other members of the school, desperately scrabbling for copy, were tempted to embellish and concoct according to their individual abilities. More than once families were set at each others' throats over deeds and sentiments which were attributed to them though never, in fact, committed or expressed. Sitting safely on the sidelines I usually derived some schadenfreude satisfaction from the fracas which developed out of somebody

153

else's indiscretion; but it never occurred to me that I might, one day, be the victim of a minor apocalypse myself.

I had delivered myself of my own pronouncement on current affairs – concocted or real I can't remember – and it was the turn of the Primary Six girl sitting behind me to shuffle to her feet. 'My mother was saying to my father last night that Mrs Macdonald is going to have a baby and she's hoping that it's going to be a girl.'

I only half heard, and it was not until I noticed the teacher's eyes flicking in my direction that I felt a lump like a hunk of cold suet pudding forming in the area of my solar plexus, and some fragment of my mind catapulted into action. There were three Mrs Macdonalds in the village! Which? Two of them had had babies in the last few weeks and I knew enough about the facts of reproduction to know that they were unlikely to be producing more in the immediate future. And that left only my mother! No quartz digital display at the Olympics could have flipped to the correct conclusion more quickly. I felt a boiling flush flood to my face and then recede giving place to cold, and then the veins on my forehead swelling in anger.

'Peggy's telling lies,' I blurted out, forgetting to preface the accusation with the customary 'Please Miss'.

'No Miss, I'm not,' said Peggy triumphantly, revelling in the fact that she had scored a palpable hit.

'Sit down!' thundered Miss Martin. And when she used that tone she was obeyed.

'It will be very nice – having a wee sister,' she said to me. There was something about the way she spoke that suggested that the news was not wholly surprising to her.

'No it won't, Miss,' I muttered, becoming aware that Gillespie was smirking with satisfaction, patently smug with revenge for the way I had ragged him when his mother had done the same to him.

'That's enough,' said the voice from the teacher's desk. 'Take out your jotters and Primary Five get on with the arithmetic that we didn't finish yesterday. Primary Six, come

154

out here with your homework compositions. And the rest of you carry on learning your poetry till I'm ready for you.'

The rest of the morning, including the eleven-thirty break is forgotten. At lunchtime I raced off home, hotly pursued by my brother who had had the news translated for him since his own English was still shaky. We burst into the house and demanded the truth from my mother in tones so rude that all we got in reply was a torrent of admonition about bad manners and an unmistakably sincere assurance that one more outburst like that and our trousers – and mine in particular – would be taken down. Dinner, as we called lunch, was eaten in silence. It was perfectly obvious that my mother had been caught completely off guard; that she was angry that the embargo she had put on her news had been broken.

It took me a long time to forgive my mother, and, for truth, I can't imagine why. Perhaps it was disappointment that she hadn't let me in on the secret herself. Perhaps it was selfishness because I had become used to our cosy menage of four and subconsciously felt my status and security challenged. Whatever the reasons, I went through the winter suffering from lapses of sullenness for which I sometimes got upbraided and sometimes punished. I had no idea when the event was due and no interest in its outcome.

Looking back, it has always been a delicate puzzlement to me how a community like ours – a community of virile ex-servicemen and red-blooded women remote from the sophistications of Barbers' and Apothecaries' shops – managed to regulate the expansion of its population in those days when Town and Country weren't planned, far less families. Certainly not every mother was so meticulously scheduled as my own, it will be remembered, who had managed to produce her first two sons at the same hour of the morning on the Fourth of July and three years apart. But, for sure, our village grew in an orderly and subtly pre-ordained way which would have delighted Mrs Indira Gandhi and puzzled the Pope.

Maybe Calum the Post had a hand in the organization of

155

things – I will never know – but he certainly had timeous intimation of every 'happy event', for the simple reason that he was our lifeline with the Manchester Emporia which supplied us with such clothing as was beyond the scope of the local handloom weavers. I have never been able to fathom why Manchester secured a virtual monopoly of our textile imports when there were drapery and napery stores in places like Stornoway and Inverness and Glasgow. But, certainly, Manchester was – and may well still be – the trading centre for the firms of J. D. Williams and Oxendale who had a hallowed place in our cotton and linen liturgy, with a Welsh firm called Pryce Jones coming a poor but honourable third like the Holy Ghost in the average prayer. Their filing systems must have been astonishingly organized; I have known of a note being sent to one of them which read as follows: 'Dear Sir (not Sirs mark you), Please send me C.O.D. a dress like the one you sent Mrs MacLean for her sister's wedding – only blue and one size larger.' And the order was satisfactorily fulfilled.

Oxendale and J. D., as J. D. Williams was popularly known, were far from regarded as totally impersonal. The letters to them frequently ended 'Hoping you are keeping well. We are all fine here despite the cold weather,' or words to that effect. Such informality did not betoken naivete; it exemplifies the breakdown which can take place in the mores of business formality in the course of a long and honourable association – the sort of burgeoning of trust which reached one of its finest flowerings in the relationship that developed between Miss Helene Hanff and Frank Doel of 84 Charing Cross Road. If Miss Hanff could keep the staff of a bookshop supplied with goodies from across the Atlantic, why should not one old lady from our parts send Oxendale a dozen eggs during the years of wartime rationing with a note saying 'Please don't tell J. D. in case he thinks you're my favourite, but the hens aren't laying well just now and I remember how kind you were with the hat when my husband was in hospital.' But the war was light years away when our village was pursuing its peaceful expansion.

156

Calum the Post enjoyed trust of a different kind. He was a local man with local friends and relatives, but he wore the King's uniform, and he had taken the King's oath which was more specific about the contents of His Majesty's mail than it was about the contents of His Majesty's van. It didn't matter, therefore, that he could probably unerringly identify what lay inside every 'plain sealed wrapper', or that he knew the exact cost of every layette and every wedding gown (they usually came in the reverse order) by virtue of the fact that all mail shopping was conducted C.O.D. But even if infant wardrobes were already to hand from previous occasions, Calum would still be privy to every impending accouchement almost as soon as the father was because it was he, after all, who, personally, conveyed every advance warning note to the District Nurse; it was a bit pointless to stamp it and have it going through the hands of the sorting office when he lived a few paces from the Nurse's cottage anyway.

It was one of Calum's standing jokes that he was a grade higher in the Civil Service than the Nurse, because he did *first* deliveries while she only did second; the point of his joke being that the nurse was rarely in attendance on primiparous occasions – they being the province of Granny, who had personal experience from bed to Z, while a spinster nurse's knowledge was assumed to be theoretical. When my own Grandmother was in her seventies I heard someone mention to her that a certain elderly doctor had a splendid record in maternity, and that he had lost only two babies in his whole career. To which the old lady replied that she had delivered more first babies than she could remember, and had lost none.

By the time that I became aware that the people of our village were busy multiplying themselves, as the Bible had it, Marks 2 and 3 were rolling off the production lines, and their introduction to the cold world was being entrusted to the Nurse who, in addition to her midwifely duties, also attended to most of the other ailments of the parish. The doctor lived in a world apart. He was regarded as belonging to the 'upper crust' society which included the landlord, the factor, the banker and one or two others who spoke English and caught salmon with rods.

The doctor's life in the Highlands and Islands has changed dramatically since the days about which I'm writing. Today it is considered highly desirable for the doctor to be a Gaelic speaker even though the vast majority of his patients is likely to be totally and fluently bilingual. He has the same status as his predecessor even though he doesn't necessarily set out to seek it. If his flock is scattered, he will, never the less, attend cases personally and be welcome, and, more than likely, he will pick up a dozen eggs or a bag of potatoes for his pains in addition to a generous mileage allowance for his car. If he is really fluent in Gaelic and inventive of vocabulary he can probably carve out a lucrative little niche for himself with the local radio station pontificating on the latest controversies anent abortion and the pill. Thanks to the traditions established by those same predecessors, however, he is less likely than his city counterpart to be hauled out of his sleep at the frivolous beck of headache or backache or wind. And no matter how remote his patch by city standards, in the event of emergency beyond his own resources he is only a helicopter flip away from one of several of the best teaching hospitals in the country. But in the year of my mother's third skirmish with maternity our temporary ambassador of Hippocrates was one of the most colourful in a long and motley line.

Dr MacBeth was generally accepted to be mad. But I think that was because of a slight misinterpretation of the word 'locum'. Or it may have been because he wore the kilt. Or, again, it may have been because of the brangle he got himself into over the birth of Murdo Mor's first and only child.

Now the wearing of the kilt was a legal offence for only a short while after the Battle of Culloden, and it is, in fact, a very practical garment at the right time and in the right place. Even the Prince of Wales wears it as a gesture to his Scottish ancestry whenever he ventures north of the Caledonian Canal. But it is not, as some people in the Home

158

Counties seem to think, the daily wear of the crofters and lobster fishermen of the Outer Hebrides, and when genteel tourists from England wear it on their occasional forays north it does not help them to blend into the local community which is, presumably, their heart's desire; it tends rather to signal them out as hitch-hikers or Americans or worse. Except, of course, for the Prince of Wales who is kenspeckle from television and is, among other things, the Lord of the Isles.

There are certain things that the kilt does not go with, and two of them are half-moon spectacles and wellington boots. So, by sporting all three while riding a lady's push-bike, Dr MacBeth was not only flying in the face of convention then, but he would be flying in its face even now.

In the normal course of events Dr MacBeth could have come and gone without our ever seeing him because he was based in Obbe some six miles to the south, and we would have had to make do with the gossip about his eccentricities which, in all consciousness, was rife enough. But then came confirmation that the wife of Murdo Mor – the much respected pillar of an older community to the north of us – was on the point of having a child. Rumour to that effect had been flying around for some time, but nobody had taken it seriously because Murdo's wife was a matronly forty-four and had survived twenty years of matrimony without succumbing to matrimony's eternal hazard. Although Murdo was called 'Mor' which means 'big', he was in fact a small, tubby man who had been some kind of commercial traveller or salesman on the mainland for most of his life before returning to his native village with, allegedly, a comfortable bank balance, and a slightly staccato self-confidence which earmarked him for the chairmanship of any small committees that might happen to be set up. Disbelief at his impending fatherhood had quickly given way to inevitable ribaldry, but that had, in turn, died down rapidly when it became known that his wife was suffering the problems that can be attendant on first pregnancies in middle age. Emotionally, the villages rallied round the couple as communities do everywhere under such circumstances, and Murdo's own conduct gained him much sympathy and support as he went quietly about his croft work and, dutifully, every Sunday paid his morning and evening visits to the little exclusive fundamentalist kirk of which he was an elder in another township. If people prayed for him, as I'm sure they did, then in all probability they redoubled their efforts when they began to see Dr MacBeth trundling on his bike to visit the expectant mother twice a week.

At last the great day came. Murdo had graciously refused all but the minimum of help from the township women who, under the circumstances, were even more willing than usual to give of their time and effort. He argued that the extra work in the house helped to keep his mind off his worry. And all the women who called on him came away full of admiration for the way in which he had made preparation for what could be the happiest or the saddest day of his life. House, bed, layette . . . everything was in apple-pie order, and, on the evening before the due day he had killed and dressed a big, fat Rhode Island Red rooster so that there would be a nourishing meal ready for his wife after her ordeal. What seemed to impress the ladies more than anything else was that he had remembered to lay in rice and onions for the chicken soup, and, in universal wifely fashion, they made comparisons from which their own husbands emerged very poorly indeed.

In the event all went well, and Dr MacBeth, with the nurse in attendance, delivered Murdo's wife of a lusty baby boy.

Over the weeks, thanks to Murdo Mor's faithful reportage, Dr MacBeth's reputation had taken a turn for the better. Apparently he had not only been diligent in his attendance – which the village had witnessed for itself – but, by the bedside, he had been courteous and comforting and exuding medical expertise. On the day itself, according to the two local women who were present, the doctor had been completely self-assured and had made light of everybody's fears. He had twinkled at them over his half-moon spectacles, making little jokes and coaxing them to teach him a word or two of Gaelic. He had turned Murdo a further shade of pale by asking him what the Gaelic was for 'twins'. And after it was all over and he had washed his hands, he had been positively expansive over a couple of very large whiskies. But the bubble burst when he was on the doorstep saying his farewells. He was bending down to put on his goloshes when Murdo sidled up to him and, apologizing for getting back to business again, said, 'Doctor – when do you think I can let her have a bit of the cock?'

The doctor shot upright – in the words of one of the women 'leaving his chin where it was'. But when he got control of it again it was to give Murdo a short sharp tongue-lashing of which the most wounding phrase to an elder of the kirk was 'disgusting old man'. The two women, who had only a modest command of basic English, couldn't for the lives of them see what was so dramatically wrong with offering an invalid chicken. The young nurse, who had been trained in a Glasgow hospital, did understand but she couldn't find words to intervene quickly enough without letting her own modesty slip. Before anybody could do anything Dr MacBeth was on his bicycle and away, leaving his Gladstone bag behind in his fluster. And the drowsy new mother in the bed wondered vaguely why everybody denied flatly that there had been a bit of a hullabaloo as the doctor departed.

The baby must have arrived at the beginning of a school long weekend because only a Primary Two bothered to announce 'Doctor MacBeth gave Murdo Mor's wife a baby.' Somebody at the back sniggered but the teacher, blushing only slightly, in her wisdom let it pass.

Chapter Fifteen

The story of Murdo Mor and the doctor went round the four townships like wildfire. The young bloods revelled in it, but, for once, they couldn't improve on it. Some of the older men, who knew only Gaelic, had to have it explained to them, and they marvelled that a great language like English could be so imprecise that one word could mean two such entirely different things. Some people were furious with doctor for even entertaining the thought that Murdo Mor could contemplate asking such an indelicate question; others thought it only poetic justice that he should have his pomposity pricked at last: he had always been only too ready to bamboozle people at Grazing Committee meetings by introducing English technical phrases into the proceedings. And, needless to say, somebody made a song which I was never allowed to hear. . . .

Unbeknownst to us, our own family was scheduled for a meeting with Dr MacBeth which had nothing to do with my mother's impending confinement, of which no mention had ever been made in the house since it had been so unceremoniously announced in Conversation. Out of the blue Calum the Post brought us the news – verbally needless to say – that Big Grandfather was going to descend on us the very next day 'for a week or two'. A week or two! My parents were completely nonplussed. For the life of them they couldn't understand why the old man, who usually timed his visits to supervise the spring work or the harvest, should decide to visit us in bleak winter. Perhaps my father was apprehensive lest his father-in-law, who was very solicitous of his younger daughter's well-being, was going to keelhaul him for putting her in the family way at a time when our circumstances were at a low ebb. Which the self-same father-in-law was quite capable of doing.

But no. The old man had come all the way to Scarista for the express purpose of consulting Dr MacBeth whom he had heard to be 'very good with feet'. Big Grandfather's feet, which had troubled him for as long as I could remember, and which he had ruthlessly exploited for sympathy, were getting steadily worse, and he was now driven to hirpling around on a walking stick. Matters had finally come to a head when he had found himself unfit to take part in the autumn round-up of the sheep on the hill, and when somebody had mentioned Dr MacBeth's hitherto unsuspected talent in pedicure he had clutched like the drowning man . . .

It was obvious that the story of Murdo Mor had not reached Grandfather, and my father, who had been sympathetic to the doctor although he had enjoyed the joke, was certainly not going to embark on stories even remotely concerned with pregnancy and birth to a father-in-law who had not yet indicated pleasure or otherwise at the prospect of being made a grandfather for the third time. Quite apart from that, the old man might have had to have the *double-entendre* explained to him, and that could have been laborious and slightly indelicate. In his youth the old man had sailed as a deck hand on rich men's yachts, and he had acquired a good working knowledge when the mood came over him, of conversational English which he was inclined to flourish by slinging into a Gaelic conversation phrases which could sometimes be slightly off-beat like 'When in Rome, do as the Roumanians do'; nobody would ever dream of correcting him.

'It's a great Christmas present your mother's going to be giving you then,' he said as he lifted my brother and myself, one on to each knee.

163

'What?' I asked innocently.

'A wee sister.'

I could feel the blood rushing to my face.

'I don't want a wee sister! I don't want anything!'

'So I hear,' he said, 'but you're looking at it the wrong way all together. Think how handy she'll be for washing the dishes and fetching the water pails! You'll be having a life of Reilly of it once she's grown up a bit.'

Before I could formulate a response to what I would normally have regarded as commendable chauvinism he turned to my father and said, 'This'll be making you get on with collecting stones for building a new house, or else putting another room on to this one.'

My father was so relieved by the old man's attitude that he decided to ignore the barbed reference to the fact that we still hadn't graduated to a stone house. Instead he came out with a remark which was news to me and completely distracted my attention from the sore subject of the new baby.

'I'm putting an extension on to this house, right enough, but it's for a loom I'm putting it on.'

'A loom!' Grandfather spluttered. 'A loom! The place is a forest of looms, and not a tweed selling anywhere. You must be out of your senses, man. You should be getting on with rearing beasts for the market; people are always going to be looking for meat and that's where they'll first start putting their money when things improve. If things improve. Most of the time I think it'll take a war to get things moving again. But tweeds! Pish!'

This was an old argument. For some reason which I've never been able to discover, Grandfather despised the weaver's trade, and he made no secret of it even though he knew that it was the profession of my grandfather on the other side. The news that we were going to get a loom of our own was exciting, and my brother and I slipped away to discuss it, leaving them to argue till such time as my mother decided to intervene and silence them.

Dr MacBeth arrived next morning. He listened to my

Grandfather's tale of woe about his feet, turning to my father now and again for clarification when Grandfather's idioms became too outlandish, and then he got down to the business of examining them. Now and again the old man winced as the doctor pressed and probed at his heels and his soles, and once in a while he let out a yelp of pain. The examination didn't take long. The doctor stood up.

'You're in a bad way right enough,' he said 'you should have been seen to long ago.'

The old man looked at my father triumphantly. At last he was being taken seriously.

'Do you know the shore here?'

The old man looked slightly taken aback, but he nodded.

'The rocky part? The skerries?'

The old man nodded again.

'Do you know the very first little bay you come to when you leave the sandy beach?'

By now Grandfather appeared to be willing to nod in response to anything, although it was beginning to look as if he wasn't really taking everything in. But he took the next bit in all right.

'I want you to go down there twice a day at dead low tide, and paddle for a quarter of an hour each time. A *full* quarter of an hour,' the doctor said emphatically. And then he added, rather unnecessarily one would have thought, 'In your bare feet.'

The doctor picked up his Gladstone bag which he had never opened.

'Make sure he does it,' he said to my father as he turned to go away.

'Don't worry, I'll make sure Doctor!' The enthusiasm in my father's voice caused the old man to glare, but he said never a word during the whole time that my father was walking the doctor down to the gate. He just sat with his hands on his knees staring down at his bare feet, and when Tiger came up to sniff at his toes he kicked him to the far side of the room.

165

'What the devil kind of a doctor is that?' he exploded when my father returned.

'He's a very brilliant man. He was in Africa for five years before he came here, he was telling me!'

'The damn sea's warm in Africa! If he thinks I'm going to make a fool of myself going paddling at my age in the middle of winter, he's—'

'Oh, you're going all right. I promised the doctor you'd do exactly as he said, and he's coming back to see you two weeks from today.'

My mother spoke for the first time. 'Are you sure he won't catch his death of cold, John?'

'Not at all. He'll have his coat and his scarf and his cap on. It'll do him a world of good. Just you wait and see.'

I had rarely heard my father so enthusiastic, and the more eloquently he waxed the more difficulty he had in keeping the smile in his eyes out of his voice. I felt sorry for the old man. I knew the exact spot that the doctor had mentioned. It had a bottoming of smooth round stones the size of a man's fist, and they were so slippery and coggly that I could barely keep my feet on them. I also knew that even in high summer the sea was icy cold at full ebb.

The voice from St Clement's bench was getting plaintive.

'One of the low tides is bound to be in pitch dark at this time of the year.'

'Pitch dark! There's a moon you could read *Cooper's Wee Red Book* by.' My father had to turn his back, and even my mother's frown was giving way to a twinkle. 'And, in any case, there's a good double-wick lantern in the byre.'

I don't know how much the doctor had enlarged on his treatment to my father when they were alone outside, but it became obvious that – funny though he might find it – father was going to make Grandfather follow the instructions to the letter. And he did. And in all fairness to him he accompanied the old man on every one of his extraordinary excursions. And within four or five days Grandfather was beginning to admit that his feet were getting

166

better. By the time Dr MacBeth re-appeared in a fortnight's time, his patient was like a man who had been given a new lease of life. He went off home with a pair of arch supports which the doctor instructed him to wear inside his shoes for a further fortnight and then throw away.

The old man never had any trouble with his feet again, and by the time the spring sheep round-up came he was on the hill with the rest. There may be more sophisticated cures for fallen arches now, but I doubt if any are more effective than the bizarre treatment doled out by a doctor who was shrewd enough to know that there was enough of a hint of witch medicine in his treatment to appeal to the hint of primitive belief in a big strong man. And it wasn't just Grandfather's feet that Dr MacBeth cured. He healed his own reputation at the same time. He didn't stay with us for long, but when he left, the money that subscribed towards his presentation was far in excess of that which the length of his service would normally have merited, and considerably in excess of what our people, in those days, could really afford.

I wonder where he came from, and where he went to – that lonely, kilted man? What was he seeking that sent him to such extremes of geography as Africa and our Atlantic village? He gave of his talent, but nothing else of himself. Never a hint of a family, or a background, or an ambition. And yet he gave us something undefinable, and something that perhaps we needed more than we knew – a glisk of colour when the world was grey, and something to talk about when conversation was growing in on itself and doubts were beginning to creep into our hopes as our hopes were beginning to fade. There were a few like that who came, usually in search of our quaintnesses so that they could write us up in books, till we began to feel that, perhaps, it might be as well to live up to the image of exotica that they so desperately sought. And in the pleasing of them we were creating the myths about ourselves that we are only now beginning to resent – forgetting that we were accessories to the forging of them.

Even had Dr MacBeth stayed on for another month or two I doubt whether my mother would have called on his services when her time came. First babies are heralded with fanfares of interest ranging from guesses at the sex to countings of the months since the wedding. Second babies are regarded as inevitable. Third ones are usually mistakes or else a frantic re-cutting of the pack in the hope of a change of suit. After two boys, the chances were that mother's third effort would result in a girl since she and father both came from mixed families, but even that prospect wasn't novel enough to tempt my grandmother south in mid-winter since her other daughter was also on the point of providing her with another grandchild nearer home. It was obviously felt that everything could be safely left in the capable hands of a new and highly regarded District Nurse who had come to us from a neighbouring island and, consequently, was a Gaelic speaker for good measure.

Not that I knew anything about what was going on. In fact I must have been singularly unobservant because I didn't attach any particular significance to the more frequent comings and goings by the neighbouring women, or even to the fact that Calum the Post brought a couple of parcels that mysteriously disappeared without their contents being divulged. I was only vaguely puzzled by a day of frenetic activity when my mother set about washing and scrubbing every inch of the house and every stick of furniture with hot water and carbolic soap. I lost track of the number of times that I was sent to the river for buckets of water, and to the end of the house for pails of peat, while my father wandered about aimlessly, filling and re-filling his pipe and being suspiciously solicitous towards us all. And all the while my mother turned mattresses, renewed blankets, and even heaved St Clement's bench away from the wall unaided in search of lurking spiders or offending dust. It was only when my father announced that he was going to milk Rosy and Spotty – the job he hated most around the croft – that I began to suspect that something highly unusual was afoot. And when he went and borrowed a neighbour's bicycle, which I had never even suspected that he could ride, I knew exactly what the unusual occurrence was going to be. It was a Saturday evening, and there was no Calum the Post to take a message to the nurse.

As it turned out, the whole event was an anti-climax. My brother and I were put to bed together on an improvised shake-down on St Clement's bench, and when I whispered to him what was going to happen we decided that we would keep watch into the night. Which we did, nudging each other into wakefulness long after the lamp had been extinguished and my father and mother gone through to the bedroom. But to no avail. It was well into Sunday morning when the clatter of the kettle on the stove jerked me back into wakefulness, and there was my mother preparing breakfast with her girth, which I had noticed for the first time yesterday, undiminished. She smiled at me. 'Sleepy-heads,' she said. 'There could have been a dozen babies arriving here during the night, and you wouldn't even have known.' It was the first direct reference she had ever made to her pregnancy and, suddenly, I felt much more reconciled to the event.

'Is it really going to be a girl, mother?'

'Even if I knew I wouldn't tell you. There are some things that are better to come as a surprise. But, in any case, nobody knows. You don't know what a lamb's going to be till it arrives, do you? And,' she went on gently, 'it's not going to make any difference to you anyway. You're always going to be the eldest.'

There was an irrefutable and reassuring logic about that which I didn't bother to try to analyse. My Grandfather's remarks about a girl 'being useful for going to the well' came back to me, and suddenly I found myself not worrying at the prospect of a new arrival after all, and even half hoping it might be a girl.

But it wasn't. And when he arrived, he arrived stealthily in the night. By Monday, although we were still relegated to the shake-down on St Clement's bench, my brother had given up the attempt to keep vigil, and we were beginning to enjoy the experience of sleeping in the living room because it meant that we couldn't be put to bed till there was no chance of any casual visitor dropping in, and father and mother were, themselves, ready to go through to bed. So, for a moment, I was puzzled when I woke to the clatter of the kettle on the Tuesday morning and found a strange woman standing over the stove making tea. Even if I hadn't seen her before, I would have known from her crisp overall that she was the District Nurse.

'Good morning, young men,' she said breezily in the foreign accent of the island of Uist. 'If you don't hurry up and get your clothes on you won't have time to have a look at your new brother before you go to school. Do you want me to help you into your trousers?'

'No!' I blurted out in horror, not knowing which emotion was uppermost – the idea of a strange woman seeing my nakedness or disappointment at the thought that the newcomer wasn't a wee sister after all. I pulled the bedclothes over my head.

'All right,' she laughed. 'I'm taking a cup of tea through to your mother. I'll give you five minutes to get washed and dressed.' I peeped over the top of the blanket to make sure that she'd gone, shook my brother awake, and we dressed more quickly than we had ever done in our lives before.

I knew that Calum the Post had come to the house with a bottle of whisky and two bottles of port at the end of the previous week, because I'd been there when my father had opened the parcel and given him a dram. But I hadn't realized that he would be the last male visitor we would see for the ten days of my mother's purdah, because, for that time, any man who chanced to come to the house, even unwittingly, would be accused of having a *bial-bangaid* – a birthday mouth – which was the phrase for a man who came to a house on such an occasion in the hope of getting a free dram. No such inhibition applied to the women who had already begun to flock to the house as we got home from school after our baptism of tauntings and teasings. They were intent on making short shrift of the port as they rattled merrily through the housework and the preparation of meals for our mother and father and ourselves. The whisky was left strictly alone, except for a token sip that my father would take every time he poured a glass of port, which he did so often that Calum had to be contacted to replenish supplies before two days were out. It was a fiesta almost on the scale of the Hen Wedding for the women-folk who, in all conscience, found few enough occasions for celebration in those lean times. As for my brother and myself, we were never so over-indulged in our lives, and my mother would have had fits if she had realized the diet of home-baked cakes, and pancakes and scones to which we were being treated. But she was oblivious to what was going on in the living room, and seemed content to remain propped up in bed, looking rested and pretty with her pink new baby almost permanently at her breast. Once or twice, when we crept in to see her, I felt the old qualms of jealousy returning, but she always went out of her way to be affectionate and friendly and make us feel that our importance was un-diminished.

In a few days the excitement, inevitably, started to ebb as the women-folk began to ease off and return to the routines of their own homes now that all was clearly going to be well. But it was still going to be some days before mother would be allowed to get up, far less be allowed to tackle the domestic chores, and it must have been a vast relief to my father when Sarah, a second or third cousin of mine, arrived at the door with a suitcase and the news that her mother had sent her to keep house for us till such time as Auntie Kate, as she called her, was well and truly on her feet again. No less relieved was the last of the neighbour women to leave. 'Ah well, that's it till the next time,' she said to my father, who looked embarrassed and tut-tutted. 'You'll be tired of a houseful of women. But you'll be having no shortage of young men around now that Sarah's here.'

For some reason I found myself resenting the prediction although I didn't understand the implication. 'Wee Sarah' as she was called because she had the same name as her mother, had always been a very special friend of mine. We had played together since I was a toddler in the Northlands. It had been to her I had run in tears when my father had drowned the kitten in that peaty pool, and my mother had failed to comfort me, that day now so long ago. Unbeknownst to anybody Sarah and I had taken a long wire and tried to hook the kitten back out without success.

She had been a regular visitor during long week-ends and holiday times while we were staying with Great Aunt Rachel and in the schoolhouse and, more frequently, since we had moved into what I still thought of as the new house. Without anybody noticing she had slipped into teenage and left school, and now here she was, a chubby little girl still in all our eyes, but brought up to be a competent housekeeper by a notoriously house-proud mother. She could even milk a cow, and that gave her extra special prestige in the eyes of my father who had secretly confessed to me that he was worried that the milk supply was going down, and that the cows would be well-nigh dry by the time my mother was up and about. But I wasn't to let on in case mother started worrying and attempted to get out of bed too soon. I understood his fears full well, and knew that it would be serious for us if we began to run short of milk in winter; as it was, Rosy was farrow and giving very little milk; and Spotty was very temperamental and didn't respond well to father's milking. That night in the byre, as I held the lantern for her, I told Sarah about my father's worries, but she tossed her head and laughed.

'It's easy to work a cow back up if you know how', she said. And it wasn't difficult to see what she meant. Unlike my father she was a two-handed milker, and though her hands were barely large enough to grasp the swollen teats, she had the true milker's rhythmic pull, and the two jets of milk alternated into the foaming pail as if they were one continuous stream; it required only a glimpse of the cow's face as she stood contentedly chewing her cud to realize that Spotty knew that she was in no danger of sudden sharp tug or nick and was prepared to let her milk flow accordingly.

Father was delighted to be able to relax over his newspaper again. And I, of course, was revelling in my continued late nights. My brother had been moved back to the bedroom where he would share the second bed with my father, and Sarah and I were put on St Clement's bench which had been widened with a row of inward-facing chairs lined beside it. The evenings went by in almost unbroken silence once my brother went to bed. Sarah had brought with her a pile of some of the comics which were beginning to find their way to the islands then – the *Beano*, and *Dandy*, the *Hotspur* and the *Wizard* – and though some of them were weeks old they were new to me, and exciting beyond description. Sarah, who had read them all several times, would help me get the serial cartoon strips and adventure stories into sequence, and we would sit, without word or sound except for the turning pages, till father finally folded away his *Daily Express* and got up to put the cat out. It was only when the bar of light showing above the bedroom door was extinguished that Sarah and I would begin to talk. She had an endless supply of stories about the boys and girls I had known, and now barely remembered, in the Northlands. Being older she was also privileged to hear some of the adult gossip, and the company of teenagers older than herself had provided her with a fund of the kind of story that parents fondly imagine only boys exchange; my father would have been more than a little astonished if he had heard some of the jokes that his innocent son was being taught to appreciate. Invariably, however, it was father's hoarse 'Shut up you two and go to sleep' that finally drew the entertainment to a close.

All too soon, the night came that was to be Sarah's last. Mother had been getting up for longer and longer each day, and she had announced that she was now ready to take charge. It was like the end of a holiday. And I knew in my heart that once mother was in full charge, there would be a period of tough discipline till she got the household moving in its normal, workaday rhythm again. For a long time after father's demand for silence I lay awake feeling slightly sad; already the first pangs of loneliness were beginning to creep in on me because I knew that by the time I came home from school next day Sarah would be gone. But tiredness was beginning to take over, and I was just dropping over the edge of the dark when I became aware of Sarah's breathing beside me. I snapped back. At first I thought she was crying and I vaguely wondered what had upset her.

'What's wrong?'

There was no reply.

'Are you all right?'

Still there was no reply, and I realized that what had brought me back to wakefulness was the heavy breathing of someone who sounded as if she had been running. Which was a ridiculous fancy. She must be dreaming.

'Are you asleep, Sarah?'

Then, so lightly that at first I thought I was imagining it, I felt her fingers touch my naked thigh. It was nothing. Just a brushing, light, passing touch that had probably happened accidentally a score of times before, except that this time something from an unknown area of instinct told me it was no accident but a signal that I understood but didn't know how to obey. I felt my chest tensing and, incongruously, something inside me going cold at the same time as a radiating heat enveloped me from the young body beside me – a body that seemed to have changed suddenly; although it wasn't touching mine, I was aware that it was full and mature in a way that I had never noticed. Then a dryness of the mouth, and something that savoured of fear. Slowly the lightly caressing

174

fingers moved upwards till they reached that part of me that nobody's fingers had ever touched before except my mother's in a clinical and altogether different way which had left no memory. And now that part of me, without my control or command, sprang into the firm grip of someone who could never again be just a childhood friend.

'Come on', she whispered. 'You know what to do.'

I couldn't move.

'Come on, I'll show you.' And I felt myself being pulled over on my side.

'No', I managed to croak hoarsely.

'What are you afraid of? Come on, it's our last chance!' and she began to kiss me on the lips.

Then something snapped.

'Leave me alone. I don't like you now!' The words came out before I could stop them and without my meaning them.

There was a sudden stillness, and an ebbing of warmth like a door opening on snow. And anger that was like a whiplash as she turned her back.

'Coward. Rotten little baby. You're not even a boy, far less a man.'

The palpable silence of a woman scorned. I lay for a time of which I have no measure, with my whole being urging me to turn to her and beg her to start where she had left off. But my tongue wouldn't say what I wanted, and my hands didn't know where to go. Sometime before morning I fell asleep, and when I woke I imagined I had been dreaming till I looked up and saw Sarah bent over the stove, her face flushed and her eyes avoiding mine. Before I could think of anything to say the bedroom door opened and my father came through. He opened his mouth to say something, and then stopped himself and looked quickly from one to the other.

'All right, Sarah,' he said briskly, 'you go and milk the cows and I'll get the boys ready for school.'

It was a long day. Since the arrival of the baby my brother and I had got into the habit of taking a sandwich to school and having 'a piece lunch' with the boys and girls who came from the far end of the township. We were doing that today, mercifully for the last time, since mother would from now on be back in command. When I got back home at four o'clock, Sarah was gone, and there was nothing left from her visit except a pile of comics on St Clement's bench. I flung my bundle of books down beside them without looking to right or to left or saying hello, and turned, and went back out.

I remember walking slowly up the path which my father had worn beside the river as he went up and down the hill each day for a sack of peat. It was the only path that led anywhere, and yet, without the purpose of the peat in mind, didn't lead anywhere at all. I had reached the boundary wall of the croft when I heard my mother's voice sharply calling me back home to fill the water pails. I turned, automatically, to obey, and I could see the village with its outline already dimmed grey in the early winter dusk, and, for a moment, I fancied that it had changed. Of course it hadn't. A village can't change overnight. But a boy can.